This Page Intentionally Left Blank

About Us

The Superintendent of the United States Military Academy (USMA) at West Point officially approved the creation of the Center for Nation Reconstruction and Capacity Development (C/NRCD) on 18 November 2010. Leadership from West Point and the Army realized that the US Army, as an agent of the nation, would continue to grapple with the burden of building partner capacity and nation reconstruction for the foreseeable future. The Department of Defense (DoD), mainly in support of the civilian agencies charged with leading these complex endeavors, will play a vital role in nation reconstruction and capacity development in both pre and post conflict environments. West Point affords the C/NRCD an interdisciplinary and systems perspective making it uniquely postured to develop training, education, and research to support this mission.

The mission of the C/NRCD is to take an interdisciplinary and systems approach in facilitating and focusing research, professional practice, training, and information dissemination in the planning, execution, and assessment of efforts to construct infrastructure, networks, policies, and competencies in support of building partner capacity for communities and nations situated primarily but not solely in developing countries. The C/NRCD will have a strong focus on professional practice in support of developing current and future Army leaders through its creation of cultural immersion and research opportunities for both cadets and faculty.

The research program within the C/NRCD directly addresses specific USMA needs:
- Research enriches cadet education, reinforcing the West Point Leader Development Systems through meaningful high impact practices. Cadets learn best when they are challenged and when they are interested. The introduction of current issues facing the military into their curriculum achieves both.
- Research enhances professional development opportunities for our faculty. It is important to develop and grow as a professional officer in each assignment along with our permanent faculty.
- Research maintains strong ties between the USMA and Army/DoD agencies. The USMA is a tremendous source of highly qualified analysts for the Army and DoD.
- Research provides for the integration of new technologies. As the pace of technological advances increases, the Academy's education program must not only keep pace but must also lead to ensure our graduates and junior officers are prepared for their continued service to the Army.
- Research enhances the capabilities of the Army and DoD. The client-based component of the C/NRCD research program focuses on challenging problems that these client organizations are struggling to solve with their own resources. In some cases, USMA personnel have key skills and talent that enable solutions to these problems.

For more information please contact:

Center for Nation Reconstruction and Capacity Development
Attn: Dr. John Farr, Director
Department of Systems Engineering
Mahan Hall, Bldg. 752
West Point, NY 10996
John.Farr@usma.edu
845-938-5206

This Page Intentionally Left Blank

Table of Contents

List of Appendices

List of Figures

Chapter 1
Introduction

1.1 Overview

The Defense Threat Reduction Agency (DTRA) is the Department of Defense's (DoD) official combat support agency for countering weapons of mass destruction that include chemical, biological, radiological, nuclear, and high explosive weapons (Defense Threat Reduction Agency, 2007). Within DTRA is the Consequence Management Assistance Program (CMAP), the DoD's primary consequence management program for the United States' partner nations (PN). CMAP was established in 2010 and is undergoing rapid development in order to become an effective organization for the DoD. The purpose of this project is to develop a framework to assess and evaluate the capabilities and capacities for each PN's consequence management program.

Currently CMAP has an unreliable metric system that fails to provide meaningful analysis to show definitive improvement in measured areas. CMAP measures over one thousand metrics for each PN, making it difficult to track progress and standardize the collection process. In addition to these problems, CMAP also faces several limitations, to include limited interaction with a PN's military personnel. This is significant because in most cases, the PN's military usually has a significant role in executing consequence management. Additionally, there is no calibrated training for the CMAP personnel who collect data. This lack of proper training combined with a large range of metrics produce an inaccurate picture of the strengths and weaknesses of a PN's consequence management program.

This research is to use value focused thinking in conjunction with the Systems Desgin Process (SDP) to create a framework that will effectively analyze a PN's capacity and capability to handel extreme crisis situations (Parnell, et al, 2010). The framework provides CMAP the ability to compare data over time and track PN progress. It allows the user to generate recommendations for the DoD on PN resource allocation in order to further develop their consequence management abilities and nurture international relations.

The goal is to develop a user-friendly framework for CMAP in order to easily assess a PN's consequence management program and track their progress over time. This system will allow a CMAP employee to easily collect and analyze PN data, and allow CMAP to successfully meet their program goals by efficiently consolidating and effectively analyzing data. The design will also solve CMAP's previous issues of data calibration and assessment uniformity by using a standardized metric system across all PNs. Combining these abilities allows CMAP to easily assess, compare, and track the progress of PN's consequence management programs. Upon completion of a PN's evaluation, the framework produces an overall score for the PN. Finally, the system is flexible and allows decision makers to change the metrics and weighting according to which PN they are analyzing.

This Page Intentionally Left Blank

Chapter 2
Literature Review

2.1 Introduction

Since the Cold War, weapons of mass destruction (WMD) have been at the forefront of foreign policy and a constant source of international tension. WMDs is defined as munitions with the capacity to kill large numbers of human beings and/or bring great damage to manmade or natural structures indiscriminately using a variety of methods. Weapons employed include chemical, biological, radiological or nuclear. While the threat of a catastrophic exchange of nuclear weapons with another major world power has decreased, the threat of WMD has risen. A policy of deterrence cannot effectively stop unidentifiable enemies and terrorist organizations from using these technologies to induce mass casualties against the US and its PNs (Betts, 1998). In particular, the threats of WMD by rogue nations and terrorist groups have increased, thus causing the US and its allies to devote more attention to crisis and consequence management (USAF Counter Proliferation Center, 2004).

Consequence management is "a process to mitigate the effects of the use of weapons of mass destruction" to include chemical, biological, nuclear, and high-yield explosives (USAF Counter Proliferation Center, 2004). One of the primary concerns of consequence management is assessing a government's ability to plan and execute an incident response that is composed of several different agencies (Center for Counter Proliferation Research National Defense University, 1999). DTRA, and CMAP specifically, have been tasked as the lead agencies by the DoD to evaluate the foreign consequence management (FCM) of PNs through the use of metrics.

2.2 Foreign Consequence Management (FCM)

FCM provides a critical role in the overall response to chemical, biological, radiological, nuclear and enhanced conventional weapons (CBRNE) incidents overseas. The US Governments' (USG) FCM program is responsible for coordinating the assistance given to PNs (Department of State, 2007)). The USG FCM program includes DTRA and CMAP, as well as many other government agencies: the Assistant Secretary of Defense; Global Security Affairs (agency for countering WMD, nuclear forces and missile defense, cyber security and space issues) (Department of Defense, Office of the Under Secretary of Defense for Policy); the Chairman of the Joint Chiefs of Staff; the Secretaries of the Military Departments; the geographic combatant commanders; the commanders, U.S. Strategic Command (USSTRATCOM) and US Joint Forces Command (USJFCOM) (Department of Defense, 2007). As a result, the planning, training, and execution of FCM operations is very difficult. Since no single agency can manage an emergency response on its own, a multi-agency effort is necessary.

FCM pertains to any international event that involves CBRNE weapons with the "potential of creating catastrophic human casualties" that may prompt a request for immediate international assistance (Department of Defense, 2007). While the USG FCM program requires the government to respond to, manage, and mitigate the effects of a CBRNE incident, the PN's government still retains the responsibility for managing the response (Department of Defense, Defense Threat Reduction Agency 1-3, 2007). If the PN requests assistance from the USG, the DoS becomes the lead federal agency in coordinating the government's response to the incident (Department of Defense, 2007). Figure 2.1 shows the coordination and communication process after a CBRNE event has occurred. After a PN requests assistance, the Department of State (DoS) and Combatant Commands (COCOM) are notified. The DoS coordinates with the National Security Staff to provide support back through the DoD and COCOMs.

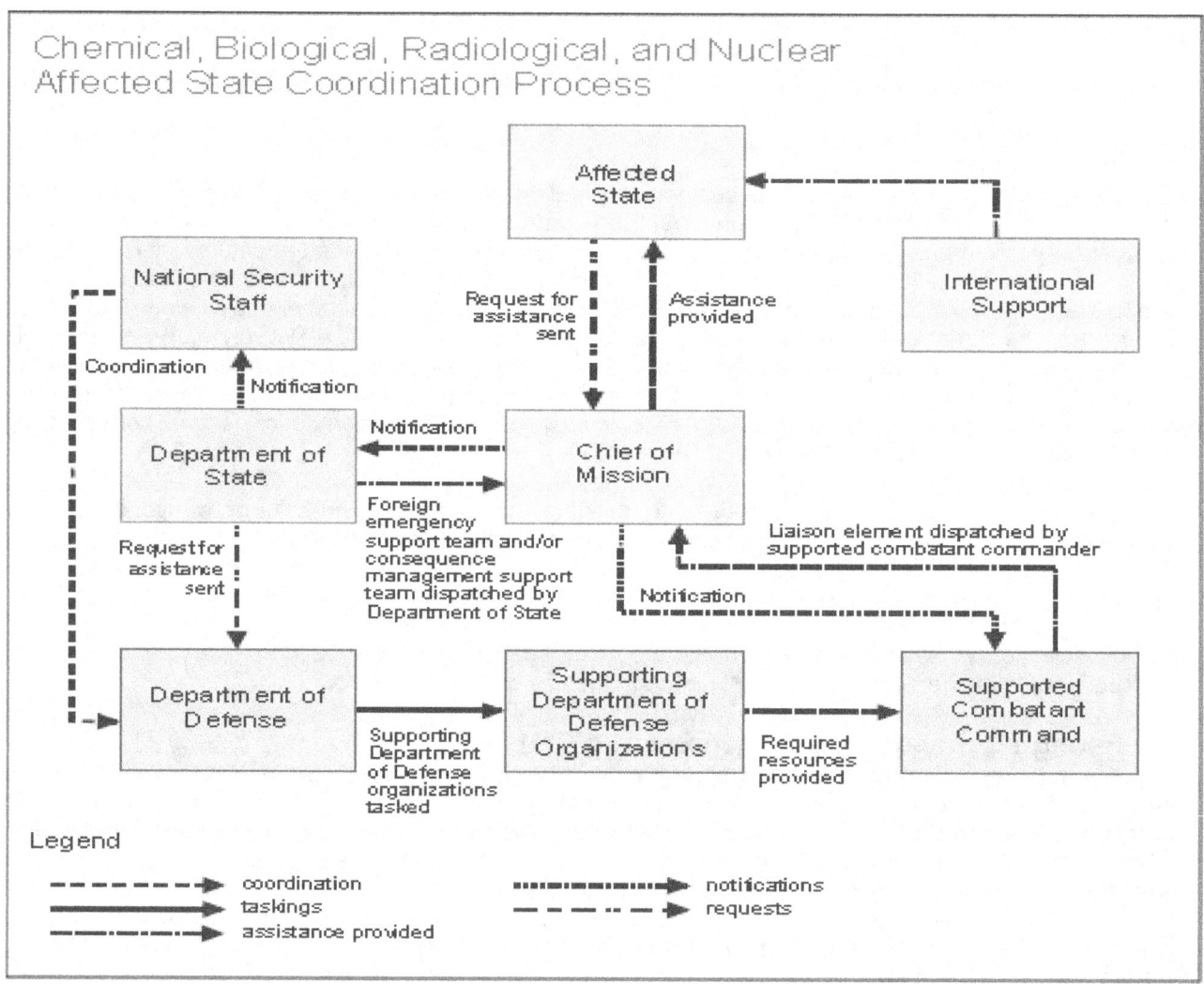

Figure 2.1 The Coordination and Communication Process (Department of Defense, 2007)

2.3 DTRA and CMAP Background

One of the primary agencies that provide aid in FCM operations is DTRA. DTRA was established on October 1, 1998 as a joint task force defense agency under the Office of the Secretary of Defense (USAF Counter Proliferation Center, 2004). DTRA's main goal is to tackle three national security issues: terrorism, improving the current capabilities of the DoD to prevent nuclear fallout, and the improvement of a nations' "nonproliferation and counter-proliferation missions" (USAF Counter Proliferation Center, 2004). DTRA's mission is to interact with foreign nations in order "to reduce the threat to the United States and its allies" (USAF Counter Proliferation Center, 2004). Figure 2.2 is the DoD organizational chart with DTRA highlighted.

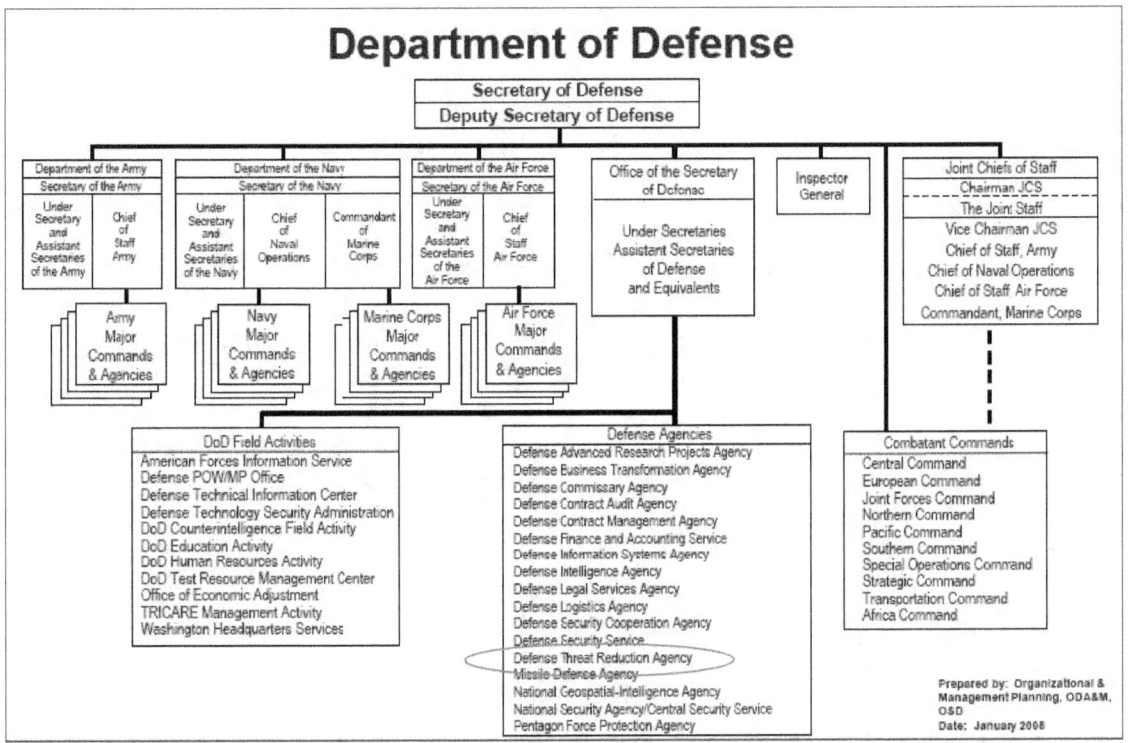

Figure 2.2 DoD Organizational Chart (Office of the Secretary of Defense, Office of the Director of Administration and Management, 2008)

As seen in Figure 2.3, DTRA provides assistance and recommendations to the geographic COCOM CDRs in order for them to increase the consequence management capability and capacity of PNs within their commands. In order to implement these changes, the COCOMs request military support for CBRNE incidents or accidents. This request for FCM operations makes its way to the Secretary of Defense for approval. As the COCOMs implement these changes, DTRA continues to assess the PNs' improvement and areas of weakness. This continuous process allows the PNs to improve their consequence management programs as well as identify where funding should be applied.

Photo Removed Due to Copyright Restrictions

Figure 2.3 *DoD FCM Process(Office of the Secretary of Defense, Office of the Director of Administration and Management, 2008)*

DTRA has been fully operational and working with the COCOMs for almost a decade, but CMAP is only a year old. CMAP's mission is to reduce threats by "cooperative threat reduction programs…and on-site inspections" (Department of Defense, 2007). Its current reduction programs and inspection system are somewhat rudimentary and are under development. In order to accomplish their mission, CMAP must help the COCOMs provide targeted consequence management assistance to PNs following a CBRNE event by improving CBRNE disaster management and interoperability with US response forces (Prins, 2012). A more deliberate and quantitative framework for assessment is necessary to accomplish this mission.

2.4 Metric Development and Framework Approach

To provide CMAP a means of measuring PN consequence management, a framework is needed to convert qualitative data into a quantitative assessment. The main focus of the framework is the development of metrics to effectively measure consequence management. Metrics are quantifiable goals that are based on expected outputs (Department of Energy, 1995). They are developed by considering two things: the stakeholder wants, needs, and desires within the organization and the organization's overall functions and objectives (National Research Council Staff, 1999). While performance metrics can be a useful tool in determining success or failure, they often do not actually measure the goals they are supposed to and have little statistical significance (Hubbard, 2007). Therefore, the development of appropriate metrics is critical. Quantitative metrics and tracking improvement over time is one of the major challenges facing CMAP. There is currently no standardized system for collecting data and assessing countries, and the metrics that do exist do not offer the user the ability to determine success or failure.

To determine the quality of a metric several characteristics are examined. First, a metric must be specific: clear and focused to mitigate confusion or uncertainty. Second, they must be measureable: must be quantified and compared to other data (Department of Energy, 1995). Marshall Meyer (2003) analyzed the failures of many business firms and other kinds of organizations and found that one of the biggest reasons they had trouble with performance measurement was because the performance they wanted to measure did not match the metrics they used with to measure that performance. Third, metrics should be attainable: measurements are achievable and reasonable under the conditions in which information is gathered (Meyer, 2002). In other words, they must be feasible. Fourth, they must be realistic: fit into the organization's constraints and are cost effective. For the metrics to be collected over a period of time, they must be sustainable. Budgets and other factors will always change, but the ability to collect metrics must be sustained.

Another consideration for this project is timeliness – metrics must be collected and used within the given timeframe. The most important part in determining the quality of a metric is whether it can be used for the collection of meaningful data for trending and analysis. Yes or no metrics should only be used when the situation involves establishing a trend, baseline, target, or start-up case (Department of Energy, 1995). These metrics are hard to analyze and measure against each other and therefore do not provide much opportunity for meaningful analysis. If qualitative metrics are used, it is important to ensure they are assigned value according to stakeholder values. Following these guidelines, even the metrics that are qualitative have a value that allows them to be compared to other metrics and measured over time. One of the ways to establish quality metrics that mitigate these problems is to create a scale where each number value has an associated description. This not only avoids the problem of having yes or no metrics, but it also gives users the opportunity to adjust their framework over time. If the metrics they create meet the above criteria and the data collection is standardized, they are able to give feedback to PNs and improve their consequence management. Ultimately, the development of these metrics can have a dramatic impact on improving a PN's ability to respond to CBRNE events and also focus US support money to very specific areas.

This Page Intentionally Left Blank

Chapter 3
Model Development

3.1 Current System

CMAP currently has an underdeveloped and loose framework of metrics to assess the performance of a PN's consequence management program. CMAP's greatest challenge in this regard is a lack of standardized assessments and quantifiable data.

The system lacks standardization because a different method of assessment is used every time a PN is evaluated: metrics are added and subtracted from the framework based on the PN's current capability and capacity. Also, there is no standardized or calibrated training for the users of the system, thus leaving the potential for error in data collection and results. Once data has been collected by the user, there is no system to store the information or to allow for analysis.

A lack of quantifiable data also makes it difficult for CMAP to measure progress over time. Each evaluation comes from an excel spread sheet with 23 sub-mission areas, several activities, with a total of 1192 evaluation metrics. The spread sheet uses a yes or no scale to evaluate each metric so that there is no quantification. The metrics do not allow for an overall score or summarized assessment which can highlight areas of weakness. The stakeholders believe that this spreadsheet is too large for this type of data collection. The shear volume of metrics cause an ineffective and inefficient means of evaluating PNs. Figure 3.1 is a Functional Flow Diagram that depicts the steps of DTRA's current system. After DTRA identifies a problem and prepares a response team to travel to the PN, the team begins their evaluation of the PN by collecting data. This data is usually collected by asking yes or no questions that pertain to the 1192 metrics. When the team completes the evaluation, they return to DTRA and conduct their assessment of the PN. This information is then shared with other agencies and feedback is given to the PN and the COCOM.

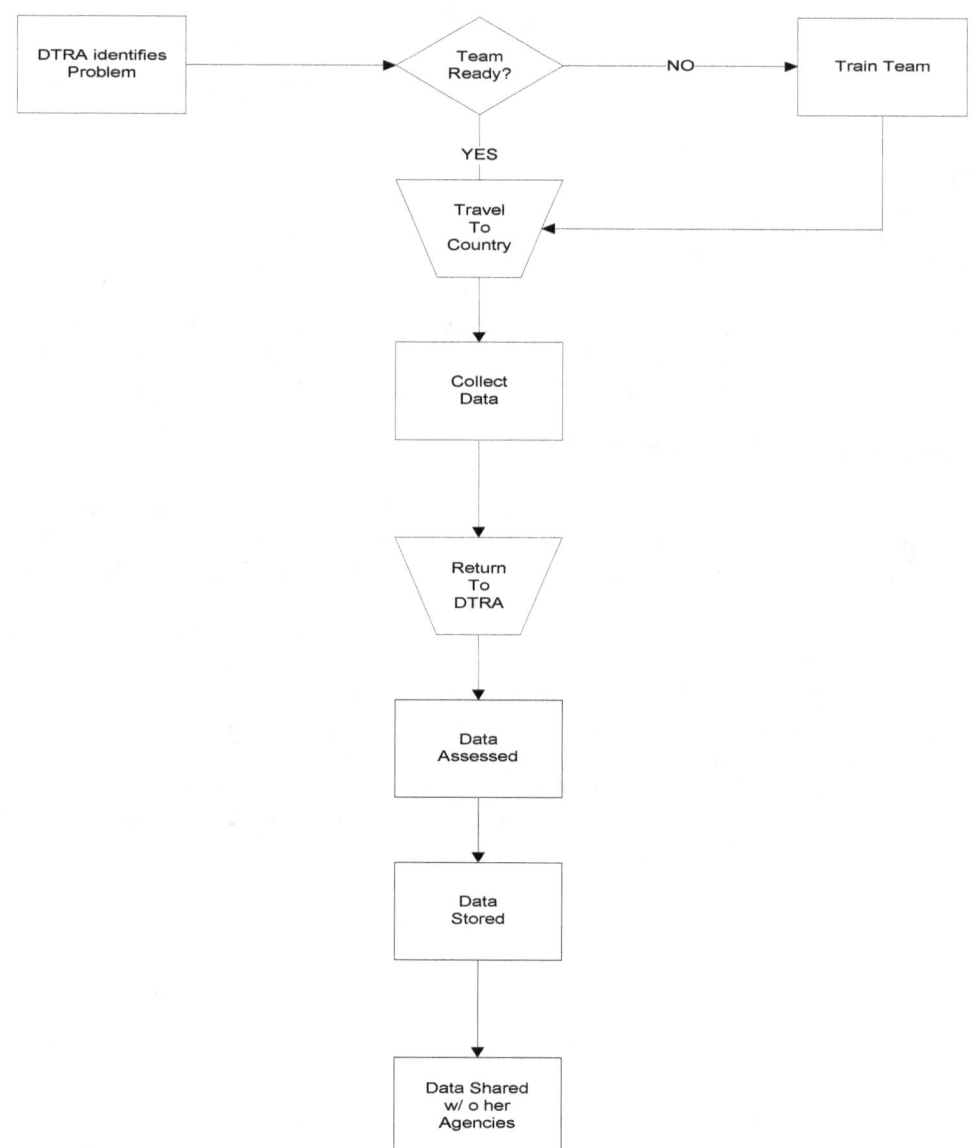

Figure 3.1 *CMAP's PN Assessment Functional Flow Diagram*

3.2 Methodology

The Systems Decision Process (SDP) is the assessment framework for this research (Figure 3.2). The SDP is a collaborative, iterative, and value-based decision process that can be applied to any system, thus making it a preferred method for solving CMAP's problem (Parnell et al, 2010). The SDP is an extremely flexible framework and tailors the wants and needs of a specific project, as such, not all of the SDP's components were used in solving the CMAP problem.

Photo Removed Due to Copyright Restrictions

Figure 3.2 *The United States Military Academy Systems Decision Process (Parnell et al, 2010)*

The Problem Definition phase of the SDP consists of gathering and processing current and background information on the project in order to better define the problem. The three tasks for this phase are research and stakeholder analysis, functional and requirements analyses, and value modeling. During research and stakeholder analysis, all background information on the project is gathered from a literature reviews, research, and stakeholder interviews. The literature review provides the necessary background information to understand the context of the problem and lends some perspective to the stakeholder. After the background information is gathered, the stakeholders are interviewed to provide further information on the actual problem at hand. Finally, functional and requirements analysis organizes and breaks down the information and data into functions, objectives, and value measures to facilitate a better understanding of the problem. The output of this phase is a redefined problem statement.

The Solution Design phase of the SDP focuses on using the products of the Problem Definition phase to create the best solution that meets all of the needs, wants, and desires of the stakeholder(s). Many different options are considered during this phase in order to come up with the best solution. In order to accomplish this, solution design begins with idea generation, which is the development of different solution parameters. After idea generation is complete, alternative generation and improvement takes place to increase the value of the alternatives that are created. When applicable, cost analysis for each of these alternatives is accomplished. The output of this phase is candidate solutions that are options for stakeholder consideration.

In order to meet the needs of this project, the final two phases of the SDP were adjusted. After the candidate solutions are provided to the stakeholder, the Decision Making Phase begins. In this phase, the stakeholders provide feedback on the model and make any necessary changes to the solutions. Through changes and feedback, the final model is improved and developed. The solution decision leads to Solution Implementation. The Solution Implementation for this project includes testing the framework and adjusting it over time. The planning, execution, monitoring, and controlling of the model is an important part of ensuring proper implementation and is the responsibility of CMAP.

3.3 Problem Definition

The first step of the problem definition phase is to define the initial problem statement. The initial problem statement is as follows: "DTRA CMAP currently has an unreliable consequence management metric system that fails to provide meaningful analysis and a means of determining definitive improvement in measured areas". The initial problem statement encompasses the first interpretation of CMAP's problem and provides focus for the project in its beginning stages. After defining the initial problem statement, research and stakeholder analysis was conducted in order to better understand and define the problem. First, a literature review was conducted on foreign consequence management, DTRA and CMAP, and the importance and development of useful metrics. After completing the literature review, the stakeholders were interviewed several times to provide current information on the problem and the system used to collect data (Appendices C.1, C.2, C.3, and C.4). In addition to stakeholder interviews, previous work from the stakeholders was reviewed in order to build a foundation for the solution design. A combination of the literature review, stakeholder interviews, and previous work on this project assisted in developing a thorough understanding of the system and its challenges.

After the research and stakeholder analysis, a systemigram (Figure 3.3) was used in order to show the interactions between DTRA, DoD, DoS, CMAP, and PNs. The systemigram shows the possible sources of the problem; how these sources affect the US strategic interest; and how they are interconnected. The systemigram allows the user to visualize the interactions of the major players and thus provides a clearer picture to help develop a more efficient solution.

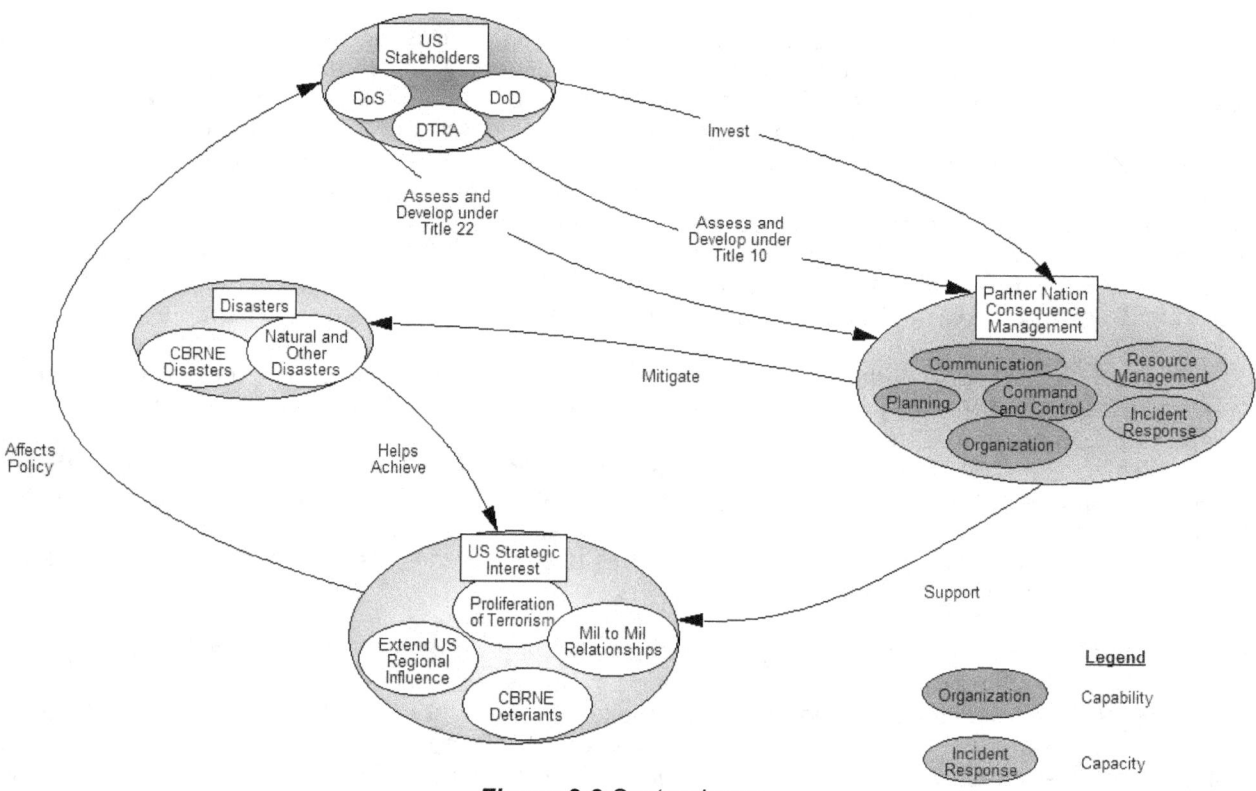

Figure 3.3 Systemigram

In order to organize all of the data collected from the research and stakeholder interviews, a functional flow diagram was created to paint a better picture of how CMAP's current system worked (Figure 3.1). A Findings, Conclusions, and Recommendations (FCR) table was developed to consolidate and summarize the major challenges associated with the current system (Appendix D). After inputting all of the research findings into the FCR table, conclusions were drawn and four final recommendations were made. The first recommendation is to take into account the need for the metrics to reflect commonalities and end states, quantitative assessment, and measureable value measures across all countries, in a simplistic framework. The second recommendation is to focus on data collection, assessment, and use. The third recommendation is to create a functional hierarchy that combines the CMAP sub-mission areas, the commonalities, and the end states that came from the products the stakeholder provided. Lastly, outside constraints such as the DoS and other agencies are considered when developing the metrics.

These four recommendations aided in the development of the fundamental objective of this project, which eventually helped finalize the redefined problem statement. The fundamental objective defines the overall function of the system and what it should accomplish. The fundamental objective is to measure the effectiveness of a PN's consequence management program using metrics, quantitative data assessment, and progression over time. Using this information, the initial problem statement was further developed into a revised problem statement: "CMAP currently has an unreliable consequence management metric analysis system that fails to provide a meaningful method for analyzing both qualitative and quantitative metrics and a means of determining definitive improvement in measured areas".

3.3.1 Qualitative Value Hierarchy
A combination of the fundamental objective, the metric breakdown (Appendix E), program focus areas (Appendix F), and activities developed by DTRA (Appendix G) were combined and used in order to develop the qualitative value hierarchy (Figure 4.2). In building the qualitative value hierarchy, two functions were created: capacity and capability. These functions were broken down from the fundamental objective and further defined in order to classify CMAP's 23 sub-mission areas. The objectives and value measures were classified and scored under the two functions of capability and capacity.

3.3.2 Capacity Function
Capacity is the extent to which a given capability can be performed, yielded, or withstood. It helps to determine "how quickly the desired capabilities can be mobilized, how much capability is available, and for how long it can be deployed" (Prins, 2012). Capacity will be measured using these four objectives: maximizing organization, optimizing planning, maximizing communication, and maximizing command and control. These four objectives are essential to maintain the capacity required to have an effective consequence management program. Maximizing a PN's organizational abilities is a key component to developing capacity, because organization is crucial to any operation and without it the PN would not be able to effectively utilize all of their resources. Along with organization comes the planning aspect of consequence management. A PN must be able to plan on both the strategic and operational level in order to employ their resources in a timely manner. The last two objectives, maximize command and control and maximize communication, increase a PN's capacity to conduct consequence management operations. Effective command, control and communications are needed in all phases of consequence management in order to further develop a PN's capacity to respond to crises.

3.3.3 Capability Function
Capability is the tangible ability to perform a function. It measures "the ability to perform a function, i.e. the type, quality, and quantity of knowledge, skills, material support, and interoperability achieved" (Department of Energy, 1996). It is important to view capabilities not as an end state, but as an interim step toward building PN capacity. Capabilities also are "the direct outputs of security cooperation activities." They should be linked to COCOM requirements and made to support the development of capacity metrics (Department of Energy, 1995). Capability is measured using two objectives: maximizing incident response and maximizing resource management. These objectives are essential in order for a PN to have an effective consequence management program. Maximizing a PN's incident response capabilities is a key component for any PN in order to effectively respond to crises. The incident response objective encompasses all the necessary tasks in order to produce an effective response to any type of crisis. The ability for a PN to maximize their resource management is also another critical capability. Without proper resource management PNs are unable to effectively support and supply the incident response operations. These two objectives effectively measure a PN's consequence management capabilities.

3.3.4 Hierarchy Development

In order to create the Qualitative Value Hierarchy, a combination of brainstorming and morphology was used to organize all of the value measures that came from CMAP's existing system. Morphology consists of combining components through the study of previous forms and structures, while brainstorming creates a pool of ideas that include the nucleus of the solution (Parnell et al, 2010). In this project, morphology was used in the creation of the value measures within the functional hierarchy. Morphology was the best method here because these value measures were derived from existing CMAP structures of stakeholder activities and sub-mission areas. After the formulation of the original value measures, brainstorming was used to create an additional objective with three value measures in order to better fully assess a PN's consequence management program. CMAP's original metrics, focus areas, and activities can be found in Appendices E, F, and G. The 1,192 metrics are not included here due to the volume.

The Qualitative Value Hierarchy was broken down into objectives and value measures (Figure 3.4). Under the capacity and capability functions, six objectives were created to further develop these two funcitons. Underneath the capacity function were the objectives: maximize organization, optimize planning, maximize communication, and maximize command and control. Underneath the capabilities function were the two objectives: maximize incident response and maximize resource management. All six of these objectives are important in providing broad measures to score a PN's capacity and capability to respond to crises. Within those six objectives, twenty-six value measures were established that encompassed CMAP's sub-mission areas, commonalities, endstates, and the 1,192 metrics.

The Qualitative Value Hierarchy provides the complete description of the stakeholder qualitative values, that include the fundamental objective, functions, objectives, and value measures. The hierarchy was then reviewed and approved by the stakeholders in order to ensure that it accurately reflected their values and needs in assessing consequence management. The clear and concise format of the hierarchy also allows the stakeholders and the user to have full traceability of the system (Figure 3.4).

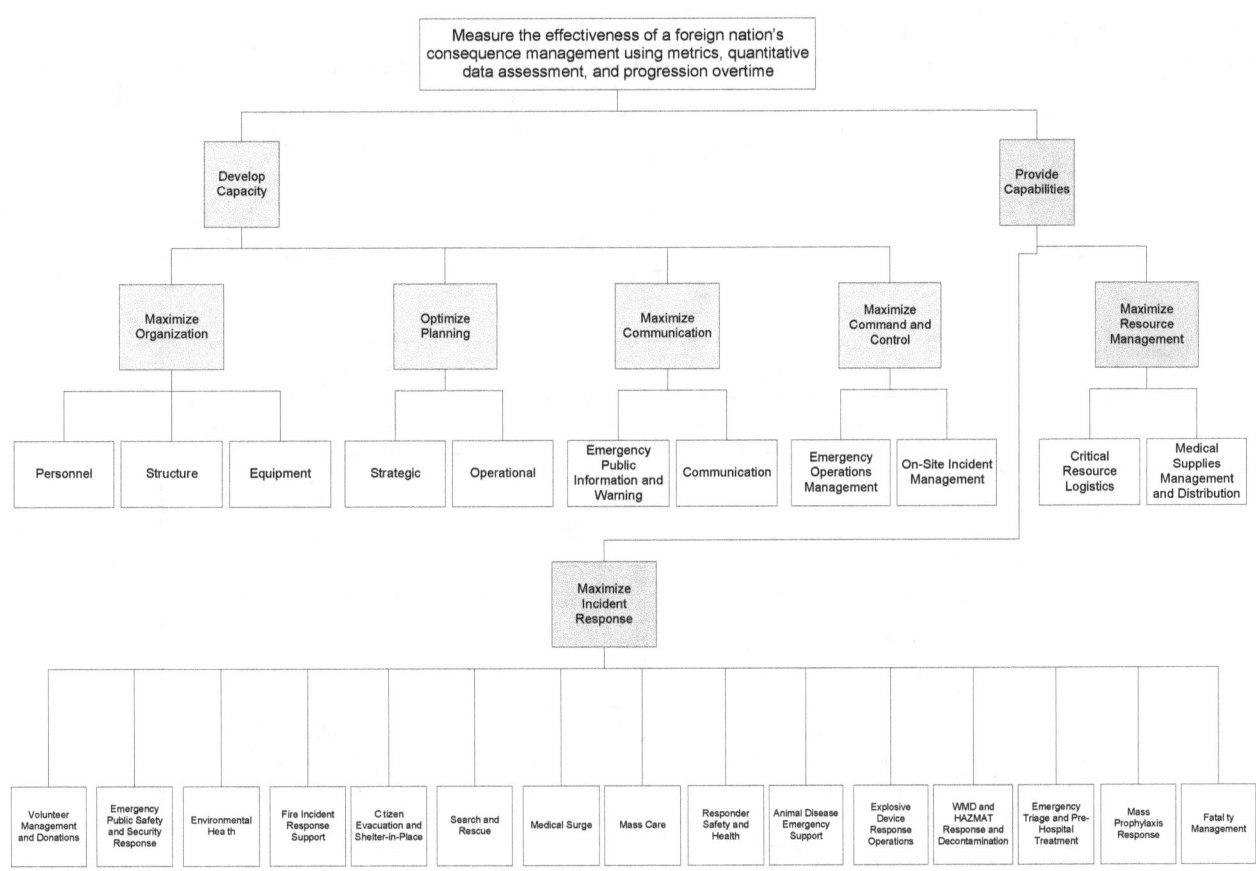

Figure 3.4 *Qualitative Value Hierarchy*

3.3.5 Quantitative Value Hierarchy

After modifying the number of metrics and fixing the functional hierarchy, each of the value measures were clearly defined and scaled. For each value measure, the 0 to 5 scales were given qualitative descriptions for each number on the scale. This allows the user to choose a numerical score for each specific value measure, thus assigning quantitative value to qualitative metrics. The scores are cumulative in nature as well, meaning the requirements for lower scores must be achieved in order for a higher score to be awarded. In order for a PN to achieve a certain score, the country must meet all of the defined qualifications for that particular score. For instance, in order for a PN to score a 3, it must have met all of the required criteria for a 0, 1, and 2 on the scale. If the PN achieves part of the criteria for a number but not all of it, the user can then give the PN an additional 0.5 on the scale. It is also important to have a way for the user to leave comments on the scoring of each value measure, so that anything of specific importance can be annotated. The individual value measure definitions and scales are available in the appendices H-L.

Next, the objectives were weighted against each other according to the level of relative importance they held within the hierarchy. Each objective was assigned a local weight between 0 and 100 with zero being the lowest level of importance and one hundred being the highest. The objective local weights must equal 100 when summed. The stakeholders then categorized the value measures within each objective into high, medium, and low categories according to the value measures level of importance. These rankings allowed the stakeholders to more accurately assign local weights according to importance. The assigned local weights numbers were assigned with the same method used for the objectives. The local weights of the value measures under each objective must equal 100 as well. For example, the value measures under Maximizing Organization must sum to 100 (EX: Personnel – 30; Structure – 50; Equipment – 20).

The global weight for each value measure is calculated by multiplying the local weights of the objectives and the value measures. The process for weighting the value measures can be seen in Figure 3.5.

Value Measures	High	Medium	Low	Local Weight	Sum
Maximize Organization					
Personnel	x			30	
Structure	x			50	100
Equipment	x			20	
Optimize Planning					
Strategic	x			50	
Operation	x			50	100
Maximize Communication					
Emergency Public Information and Warning	x			50	
Communication	x			50	100
Maximize Command and Control					
Emergency Operations Center Management	x			60	
Onsite Incident Management		x		40	100
Maximize Incident Response					
Volunteer Management and Donations			x	3	
Emergency Public Safety and Security Response		x		5	
Environmental Health		x		5	
Fire Incident Response Support			x	5	
Citizen Evacuation and Shelter-in-Place			x	5	
Search and Rescue		x		8	
Medical Surge		x		8	
Mass Care		x		8	100
Responder Safety and Health	x			10	
Animal Disease Emergency Support			x	5	
Explosive Device Response Operations		x		5	
WMD and HAZMAT Response and Decontamination	x			10	
Emergency Triage and Prehospital Treatment	x			10	
Mass Prophylaxis Response		x		5	
Fatality Management		x		8	
Maximize Resource Management					
Critical Reponse Logistics			x	50	
Medical Supplies Management and Distribution			x	50	100

Figure 3.5 Value Measure Weighting

Upon completion of the Value Hierarchy, the problem definition phase was complete. The redefined problem statement was the resulting output of this phase that provided a more in-depth analysis of CMAP's problem and set the foundation for the Soultion Design phase. The redefined problem statement is to create a framework to assess and evaluate the capabilities and capacities for each PN within a centralized military authority. This framework is an assessment of broad metrics that can be measured across PNs and time.

3.4 Solution Design

In the Solution Design phase, idea generation was used to create an Excel based model that met the needs of the redefined problem statement. The model uses the qualitative and quantitative value hierarchies as the basis for the assessment. The model uses the value measure scores to calculate a total overall assessment score for a PN. The model consists of a multiple user input page, a scoring page, and an evaluation page that allows the user to assess and score a PN. This model gives stakeholders the ability to quantitatively assess a PN's consequence management capacity and capabilities and provides an in-depth analysis of the PN's strengths and weaknesses. The excel model is the candidate solution produced from the Problem Definition and Solution Design Phases.

3.5 Decision Making

After the first model was created, it was reviewed by the stakeholders to confirm the accuracy of the local weights for the objectives and value measures as well as making recommendations on the format and usability of the model. Also, the stakeholders provided input on how the model could better meet their needs by adding additional capabilities. After an initial trial run of the model, the stakeholders added a multiple users input page, as well as other minor adjustments to increase the model's usability and functionality. To ensure that the users of the model did not change certain portions of the excel spreadsheet; pages were protected so that only the users with a password could adjust it. These decisions allowed for the creation of the best possible candidate solution that met the needs, wants, and desires of the stakeholders.

3.6 Solution Implementation

The Solution Implementation phase of the SDP refers to CMAP's application of this framework to evaluations of PNs. CMAP can use this framework to track a PN's progress over time or compare PNs to one another. Calibrated training for CMAP employees will allow them to accurately collect and standardize the data by limiting employee bias. This model will serve as CMAP's baseline framework for their PN evaluations, and the model will continue to develop further as CMAP uses the model. This evaluation system has the potential to be used by other agencies within the DTRA and even the DoD.

This Page Intentionally Left Blank

Chapter 4
Model

4.1 Model

The Partner Nation Evaluation Model transforms qualitative data collected by trained DTRA personnel into quantitative data that can be understood by stakeholders and users. The use of value measure scoring, local weights, and global weights convert the qualitative data into meaningful quantitative measures that aid in the assessment of the overall PN assessment. The model includes an evaluation page and an archive page that gives the user an in depth analysis of a PN's strengths and weaknesses while also tracking that PN's progress over time. The model is simple to understand and can be updated and modified as needed. A user guide for model use is included in Appendix M.

4.1.1 Input Page

To begin an evaluation, the user will give each value measure a score ranging from 0 to 5 based on the scale for that value measure. There are two ways to run the evaluation correctly. If there are multiple personnel inputting data that has been collected over a period of time, they will begin by putting all of the data into the "Multiple Inputs" page (Figure 4.1). The purpose of the "Multiple Inputs" page is to get an average score for each of the value measures so that the data collected during the engagement is not reliant on a single user's evaluation. If there is only one person collecting data for a PN, they will enter the data directly into the "Input Scores" page of the model (Figure 4.2). As the user scrolls over each value measure in the score column, the value measure definition and subsequent scale appears in a comment box next to the "score" column. The user then chooses the score for that value measure using the drop down menu. After all of the scores and comments are entered into the "Input Scores" page, the user then moves on to the "Calculations" or "Evaluations" page to view the assessment results.

Engagement Location Average Scores from 10 users over a period of 10 days												
	Value Measures	Day 1	Day 2	Day 3	Day 4	Day 5	Day 6	Day 7	Day 8	Day 9	Day 10	Average
Maximize Organization	Personnel	1.0	1.0	1.0	1.0	1.0	1.0	1.0	1.0	1.0	1.0	1.0
	Structure	2.0	2.0	2.0	2.0	2.0	2.0	2.0	2.0	2.0	2.0	2.0
	Equipment	3.5	3.5	3.5	3.5	3.5	3.5	3.5	3.5	3.5	3.5	3.5
Optimize Planning	Strategic	2.0	2.0	2.0	2.0	2.0	2.0	2.0	2.0	2.0	2.0	2.0
	Operation	1.5	1.5	1.5	1.5	1.5	1.5	1.5	1.5	1.5	1.5	1.5
Maximize Communication	Emergency Public Information and Warning	5.0	5.0	5.0	5.0	5.0	5.0	5.0	5.0	5.0	5.0	5.0
	Communication	2.5	2.5	2.5	2.5	2.5	2.5	2.5	2.5	2.5	2.5	2.5
Maximize Command and Control	Emergency Operations Center Management	2.0	2.0	2.0	2.0	2.0	2.0	2.0	2.0	2.0	2.0	2.0
	Onsite Incident Management	3.0	3.0	3.0	3.0	3.0	3.0	3.0	3.0	3.0	3.0	3.0
Maximize Incident Response	Volunteer Management and Donations	1.0	1.0	1.0	1.0	1.0	1.0	1.0	1.0	1.0	1.0	1.0
	Emergency Public Safety and Security Response	0.5	0.5	0.5	0.5	0.5	0.5	0.5	0.5	0.5	0.5	0.5
	Environmental Health	1.5	1.5	1.5	1.5	1.5	1.5	1.5	1.5	1.5	1.5	1.5
	Fire Incident Response Support	1.5	1.5	1.5	1.5	1.5	1.5	1.5	1.5	1.5	1.5	1.5
	Citizen Evacuation and Shelter-in-Place	0.5	0.5	0.5	0.5	0.5	0.5	0.5	0.5	0.5	0.5	0.5
	Search and Rescue	0.5	0.5	0.5	0.5	0.5	0.5	0.5	0.5	0.5	0.5	0.5
	Medical Surge	1.5	1.5	1.5	1.5	1.5	1.5	1.5	1.5	1.5	1.5	1.5
	Mass Care	3.0	3.0	3.0	3.0	3.0	3.0	3.0	3.0	3.0	3.0	3.0
	Responder Safety and Health	4.5	4.5	4.5	4.5	4.5	4.5	4.5	4.5	4.5	4.5	4.5
	Animal Disease Emergency Support	4.5	4.5	4.5	4.5	4.5	4.5	4.5	4.5	4.5	4.5	4.5
	Explosive Device Response Operations	5.0	5.0	5.0	5.0	5.0	5.0	5.0	5.0	5.0	5.0	5.0
	WMD and HAZMAT Response and Decontamination	0.5	0.5	0.5	0.5	0.5	0.5	0.5	0.5	0.5	0.5	0.5
	Emergency Triage and Prehospital Treatment	1.5	1.5	1.5	1.5	1.5	1.5	1.5	1.5	1.5	1.5	1.5
	Mass Prophylaxis Response	2.0	2.0	2.0	2.0	2.0	2.0	2.0	2.0	2.0	2.0	2.0
	Fatality Management	3.0	3.0	3.0	3.0	3.0	3.0	3.0	3.0	3.0	3.0	3.0
Maximize Resource Management	Critical Response Logistics	4.5	4.5	4.5	4.5	4.5	4.5	4.5	4.5	4.5	4.5	4.5
	Medical Supplies Management and Distribution	4.5	4.5	4.5	4.5	4.5	4.5	4.5	4.5	4.5	4.5	4.5

Figure 4.1 "Multiple Users Input" Page

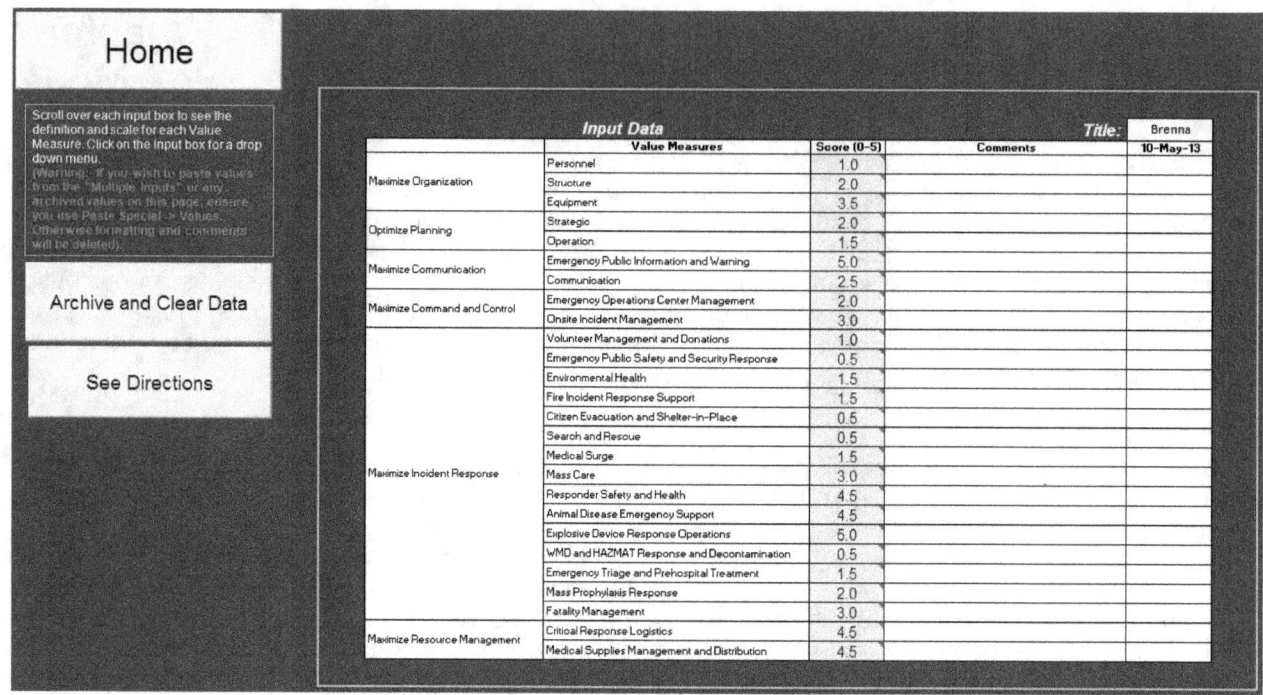

Figure 4.2 "Input Scores" Page

4.3.2 Calculations

Once the data for all of the value measures is placed into the "Input Scores" page, the calculations will run automatically and populate the overall score for that value measure. The math behind the model begins by converting the raw data score into the value from the value measure tables. That value is then multiplied by the local objective weight that it falls under. The new value is then multiplied by the local weight of that individual value measure. For example, if a PN receives a score of four for the personnel value measure, it will receive a value of 85 based on the scale created by the stakeholders (Figure 4.3). Next, the value is multiplied by 7%, which is the local weight of the Maximize Organization objective. Lastly, this value is multiplied by 30%, the local weight of the Personnel value measure, for a final value of 1.785 (Figure 4.4). The same process is used to find the value for each of the twenty-six value measures. Following these multiplications, the individual values are summed together and divided by the ideal score to obtain the overall PN score out of 100. These values are divided in case some of the value measures are not being assessed. The entire "Calculations" page where these calculations take place is seen in Figures 4.5 and 4.6.

Personnel	
Score	Values
0	0
1	25
2	50
3	67
4	85
5	100

Figure 4.3 Scale Values and Scores

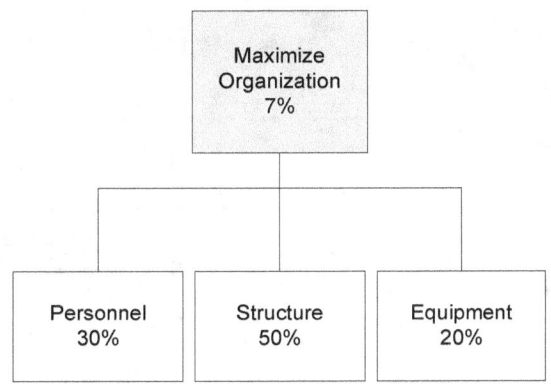

Figure 4.4 *Value Hierarchy with Normalized Weights*

1) The value of 5.95 x 0.30(the % from Personnel Value Measure) = 1.785
2) The value of 85 x 0.07(the % from Max Organization) = 5.95

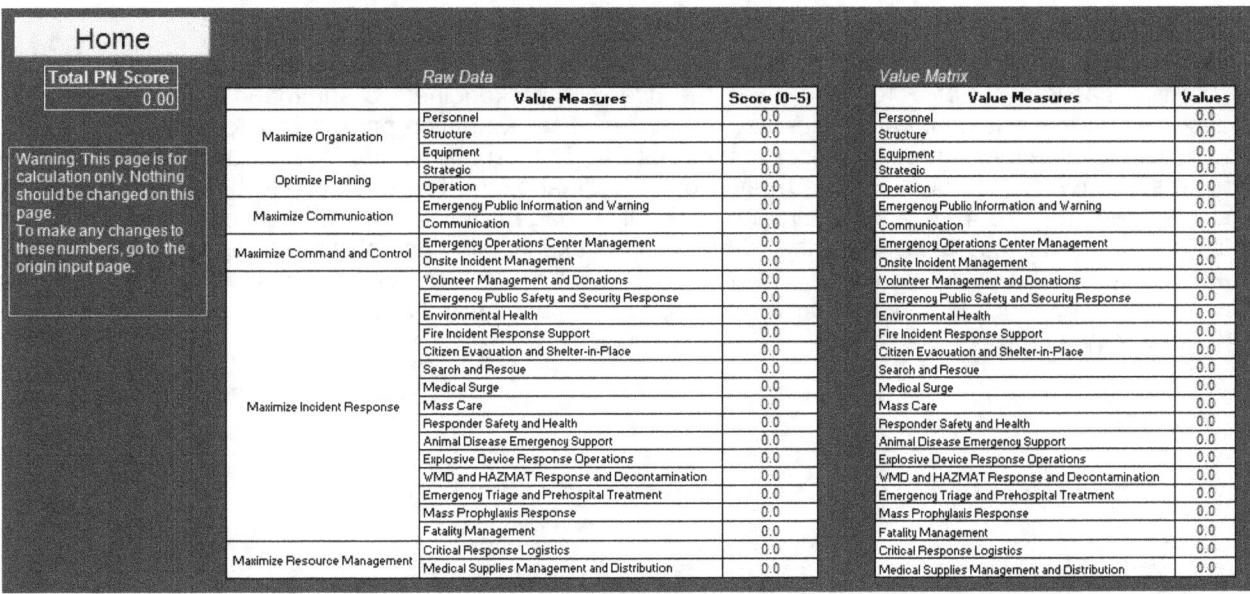

Figure 4.5 *"Calculations" Page*

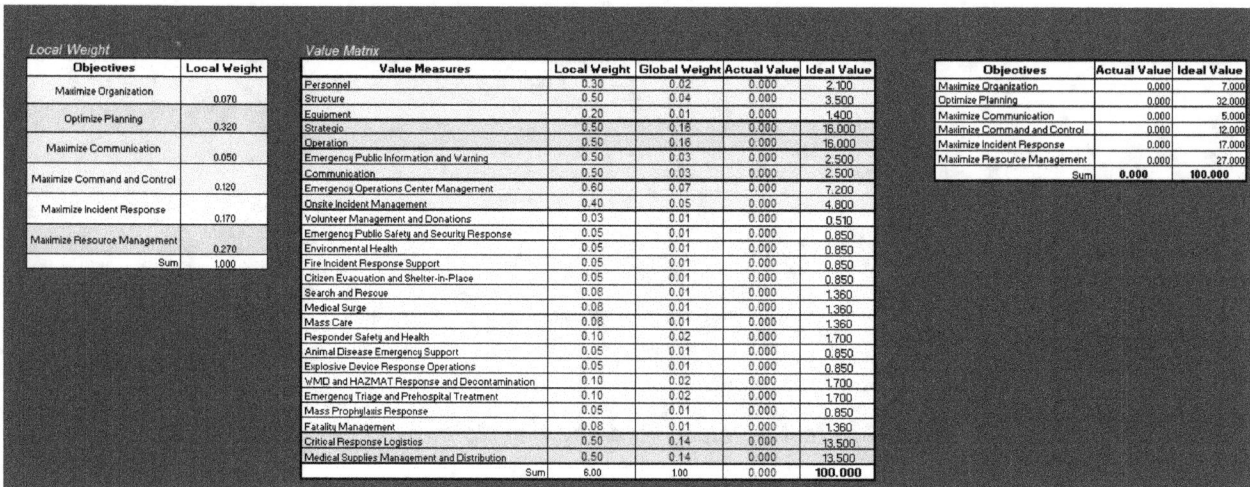

Figure 4.6 "Calculations" Page

4.3.3 Evaluation Page

The evaluation page of the model displays the overall PN score that stems from the user(s) inputs. This score is measured out of a 100 and gives the user and stakeholders a summary of the PN's current consequence management capabilities and capacities. The evaluation page also allows DTRA to locate the deficient value measures and objectives for that PN. The bar chart and the radar diagrams display the actual score (what the country scored) and compares that to the ideal score (the best a country could have scored) (Figure 4.7). Additionally, the evaluation page provides more traceability with the "Input Minimum Percentages" tables. With these tables, the stakeholders can establish a threshold or minimum percentage that the value measures and objectives must meet. If the value measures do not meet this baseline requirement, the underperforming component will appear red and allow the user to quickly locate the deficiency (Figure 4.8).

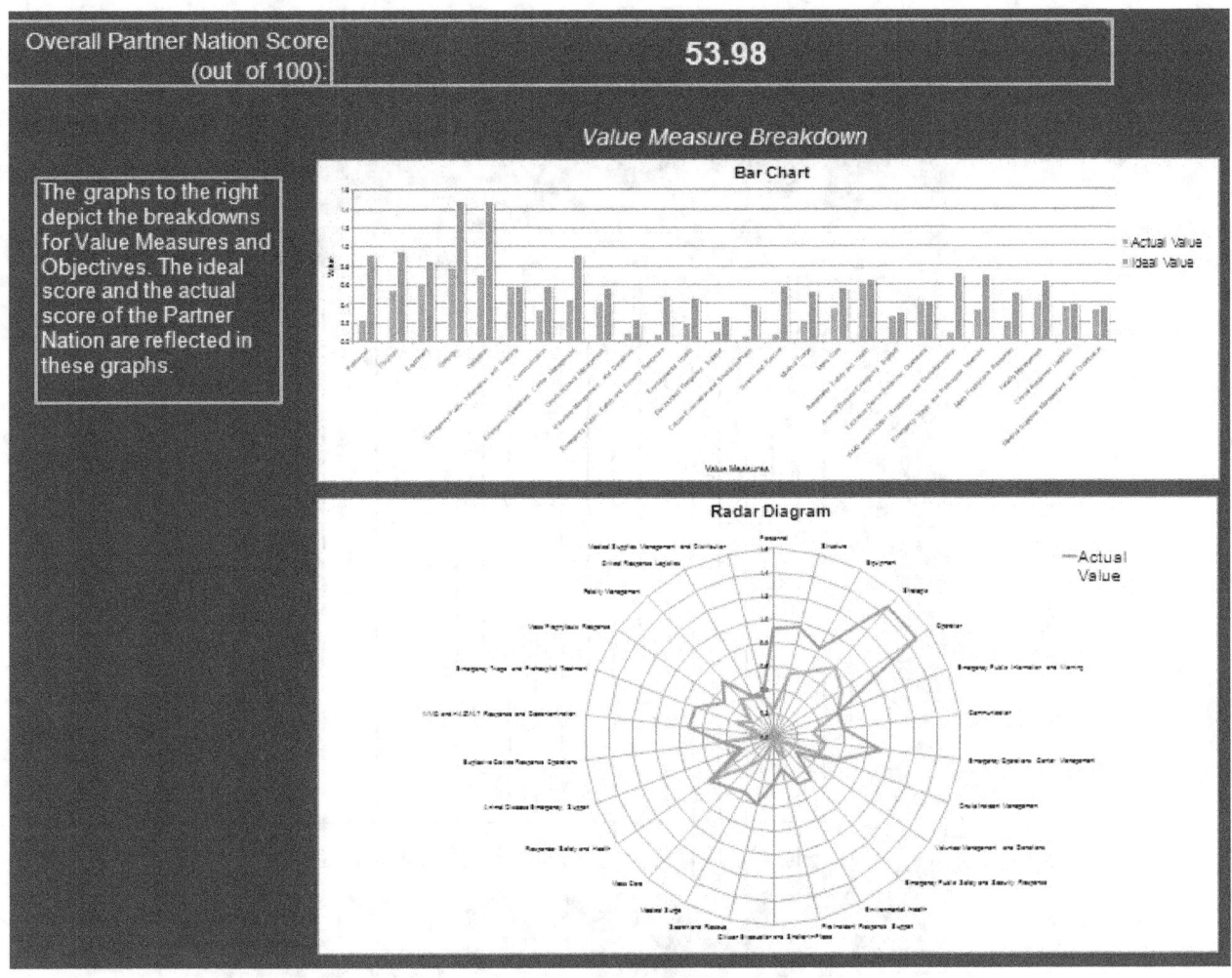

Figure 4.7 *Evaluation Page – Bar Chart, Radar Diagram, and Overall Partner Nation Score*

In order to identify the value measure and objective/areas of weakness, enter the minimum percentage in the orange boxes provided. After inputting, the minimum desired percentage/the areas of weakness will

Input Minimum Percentage: 60

Value Measures	Z-Score
Personnel	25.0
Structure	56.0
Equipment	73.5
Strategic	53.0
Operation	47.5
Emergency Public Information and Warning	100.0
Communication	56.5
Emergency Operations Center Management	48.0
Onsite Incident Management	73.0
Volunteer Management and Donations	37.0
Emergency Public Safety and Security Response	14.5
Environmental Health	42.0
Fire Incident Response Support	41.5
Citizen Evacuation and Shelter-in-Place	14.0
Search and Rescue	14.0
Medical Surge	34.5
Mass Care	62.0
Responder Safety and Health	94.5
Animal Disease Emergency Support	88.5
Explosive Device Response Operations	100.0
WMD and HAZMAT Response and Decontamination	14.0
Emergency Triage and Prehospital Treatment	47.5
Mass Prophylaxis Response	43.0
Fatality Management	67.0
Critical Response Logistics	94.5
Medical Supplies Management and Distribution	94.5

Input Minimum Percentage: 50

Objectives	Z-Score
Maximize Organization	51.0
Optimize Planning	50.3
Maximize Communication	78.3
Maximize Command and Control	57.6
Maximize Incident Response	47.6
Maximize Resource Management	94.5

Figure 4.8 *Evaluation Page – Minimum Input Percentage Tables*

4.3.4 Archive Page

The Archive Page (see Figure 4.9) of the model contains the data of previous evaluations. This page serves as the database for the Partner Nation Evaluation Model. It contains the date of the evaluation, the overall score that the PN achieved, the individual value measure scores, and any comments that the user might have inputted at the time of the assessment. This page allows DTRA to track the progress of PNs and compare their capabilities and capacities over time.

Home

To add to the archives, go to the "Input Scores" Page and click the "Archive and Clear" button. Input the date after running the macro

[Note: This page will not work if it is protected. Please do not change anything on this page. If you wish to copy any of the values archived, ensure you use Paste Special > Values].

Date	28-Feb-13	
PN Score	57.29	

Value Measures	Score (0-5)	Comments
Personnel	N/A	No personnel have received training.
Structure	2.0	0
Equipment	3.5	Not all equipment is maintained.
Strategic	2.0	0
Operation	1.5	0
Emergency Public Information and Warning	5.0	0
Communication	2.5	0
Emergency Operations Center Management	2.0	0
Onsite Incident Management	3.0	0
Volunteer Management and Donations	1.0	0
Emergency Public Safety and Security Response	0.5	0
Environmental Health	1.5	0
Fire Incident Response Support	1.5	0
Citizen Evacuation and Shelter-in-Place	0.5	Missing doctrine for emergency shelter contingencies.
Search and Rescue	N/A	0
Medical Surge	1.5	0
Mass Care	3.0	0
Responder Safety and Health	4.5	0
Animal Disease Emergency Support	4.5	0
Explosive Device Response Operations	5.0	0
WMD and HAZMAT Response and Decontamination	0.5	0
Emergency Triage and Prehospital Treatment	1.5	0
Mass Prophylaxis Response	2.0	0
Fatality Management	3.0	No exercises are conducted.
Critical Response Logistics	4.5	0
Medical Supplies Management and Distribution	4.5	0

Date	20-Feb-13	
PN Score	53.98	

Value Measures	Score (0-5)	Comments
Personnel	1.0	0
Structure	2.0	0
Equipment	3.5	0
Strategic	2.0	0
Operation	1.5	0
Emergency Public Information and Warning	5.0	0
Communication	2.5	0
Emergency Operations Center Management	2.0	0
Onsite Incident Management	3.0	0
Volunteer Management and Donations	1.0	0
Emergency Public Safety and Security Response	0.5	0
Environmental Health	1.5	0
Fire Incident Response Support	1.5	0
Citizen Evacuation and Shelter-in-Place	0.5	0
Search and Rescue	0.5	0
Medical Surge	1.5	0
Mass Care	3.0	0
Responder Safety and Health	4.5	0
Animal Disease Emergency Support	4.5	0
Explosive Device Response Operations	5.0	0
WMD and HAZMAT Response and Decontamination	0.5	0
Emergency Triage and Prehospital Treatment	1.5	0
Mass Prophylaxis Response	2.0	0
Fatality Management	3.0	0
Critical Response Logistics	4.5	0
Medical Supplies Management and Distribution	4.5	0

Figure 4.9 Archives Page

Chapter 5
Summary

5.1 Summary

The Partner Nation Evaluation Model framework is used to measure, track, and identify areas of weakness within the PN's consequence management program. The need for this framework comes from CMAP's current challenge of an unreliable metric system that fails to provide meaningful analysis to show definitive improvement in measured areas.

Using this model framework, CMAP is able to convert the qualitative data collected during PN evaluations into quantitative data that makes the goal of maximizing the capacity and capability possible. Multiple objective decision analysis and objective and value measures creation are the foundation of the metric analysis framework. Each value measure is defined with a scale to allow the data collector to easily classify the status of the PN in each category. When the data is collected accurately the six objectives and twenty-six value measures provide a PN with an accurate score that can be tracked over time. The overall score effectively captures the capacities and capabilities of a measured PN.

The flexibility of the model allows DTRA to incorporate the process into other programs as well. Pilot evaluations have begun within months of the model being developed. The model is being expanded to allow COCOM CDRs to conduct regional analysis of PNs that are under their command.

5.2 Future Research

After each evaluation, a statistical analysis (to include propagation of error) can be completed to give a more in-depth analysis of the accuracy of the evaluation. In the future a database should be created in order to organize the evaluations and provide the COCOMs data for their focus region. Another useful tool that should be developed in the future is a collection system or application to increase usability and allow CMAP data collectors to easily input data into the model while in the field.

5.3 Acknowledgments

This work was funded by the Defense Threat Reduction Agency (DTRA) as part of the Consequence Management Strategic Engagement Branch development. LTC Rob Prins was the point of contact at DTRA. The goal of the DTRA consequence management assessment program (CMAP) is assessing a PNs ability to plan and execute an incident response that is composed of several different agencies. DTRA and CMAP specifically, have been tasked as the lead agencies by the DoD to evaluate the foreign consequence management (FCM) of PNs through the use of metrics.

Chapter 6
References

Bennett, Bruce W., and Richard A. Love. "Initiatives and Challenges in Consequence Management after a WMD Attack." USAF Counter Proliferation Center, Aug. 2004. http://www.au.af.mil/au/awc/awcgate/cpc-pubs/love.pdf.

Betts, Richard K. "The New Threat of Mass Destruction." *Council on Foreign Relations*, January 1998. http://www.foreignaffairs.com/articles/53599/richard-k-betts/the-new-threat-of-mass-destruction.

Center for Counter Proliferation Research National Defense University. *Consequence Management in Need of a Timeout*. By Scott R. Taylor, Amy M. Rowe, and Brian M. Lewis. 51st Communications Squadron. Washington, D.C.: Summer 1999. http://www.dtic.mil/cgi-bin/GetTRDoc?Location=U2&doc=GetTRDoc.pdf&AD=ADA426663.

Defense Threat Reduction Agency. *Defense Threat Reduction Agency & USSTRATCOM Center for Combating WMD*. Last modified 2007. Accessed January 2013. http://www.dtra.mil/.

Department of Energy. Defense Programs and Operating Experience, Analysis, and Feedback. *How to Measure Performance: A Handbook of Techniques and Tools*. Oak Ridge Associated Universities, 1995. Accessed 6 Sept. 2012. *JSTOR*. http://www.orau.gov/pbm/handbook/handbook_all.pdf.

Department of Defense. Defense Threat Reduction Agency. *Foreign Consequence Management: Legal Desk book*, 2007.

Hubbard, Douglas W. *How to Measure Anything: Finding the Value of "intangibles" in Business*. Hoboken, NJ: John Wiley & Sons, 2007.

Meyer, Marshall W. *Rethinking Performance Measurement: Beyond the Balanced Scorecard*. Cambridge, UK: Cambridge UP, 2002.

National Research Council Staff. *Industrial Environmental Performance Metrics: Challenges and Opportunities*. Washington, DC: National Academy, 1999.

Office of the Chairman of the Joint Chiefs of Staff. *Chemical, Biological, Radiological, and Nuclear Consequence Management*. By William E. Gortney. 21 June 2012.

Office of the Secretary of Defense. Office of the Director of Administration and Management. *Organization of the Department of Defense*, 2008. http://odam.defense.gov/omp/Library/DoD_Organizational_Charts/DoD_Organization_March_2012.pdf.

Parnell, Gregory S., Patrick J. Driscoll, and Dale L. Henderson. *Decision Making in Systems Engineering and Management*. Second Edition. New York: John Wiley and Sons, 2010.

Prins, Robert. *CMAP 101 PowerPoint Brief: June 2012 Mission Statement*.

Prins, Robert. *Definitions of Capabilities and Capacities*. Building Partner Capabilities for Coalition Operations: RAND Report. 2012.

United States Congress. House Committee on the Judiciary, Subcommittee on Crime, Terrorism, and Homeland Security. *Homeland Security : The Balance between Crisis and Consequence Management through Training and Assistance*. Washington D.C.: U.S. G.P.O., 2004.

Appendix A
Annotated Bibliography

Bennett, Bruce W., and Richard A. Love. USAF Counter Proliferation Center. Future Warfare Series No. 26. *Initiatives and Challenges in Consequence Management after a WMD Attack*. August 2004, http://www.au.af.mil/au/awc/awcgate/cpc-pubs/love.pdf.
The article describes the importance of counter proliferation, the definition of consequence management, and the formation of DTRA. The article defines consequence management as the "process to mitigate the effects of the use of weapons of mass destruction." The increase in threat from the WMDs in foreign nations increased the importance of counter proliferation in the modern world and as a result, DTRA was formed. The article, also, provided background information on DTRA and the purpose that the agency serves for the United States government.

Betts, Richard K. "The New Threat of Mass Destruction." *Council on Foreign Relations*, January 1998. http://www.foreignaffairs.com/articles/53599/richard-k-betts/the-new-threat-of-mass-destruction.
This article describes the development of weapons of mass destruction. It has been traced back to the Cold War Era but this article also states the development of chemical and biological weapons. The introduction of such weapons created the concept of mass destruction rather than "complete annihilation." With this, counter proliferation became more important in the modern world and this article emphasizes the importance of agencies such as DTRA in stopping the spread of such weapons.

Defense Threat Reduction Agency. *Defense Threat Reduction Agency & USSTRATCOM Center for Combating WMD*. Last modified 2007. Accessed January 2013. http://www.dtra.mil/.
The DTRA website displays the core mission for the agency. The website provides pictures of current DTRA global operations and the PNs they are working with. Since the model is designed for this agency, the website provides good background information and stakeholder research materials.

Department of Energy. Defense Programs and Operating Experience, Analysis, and Feedback. *How to Measure Performance: A Handbook of Techniques and Tools*. Oak Ridge Associated Universities, 1995. Accessed 6 Sept. 2012. *JSTOR*. http://www.orau.gov/pbm/handbook/handbook_all.pdf.
The handbook provides the definition of metrics and the characteristics behind a high quality metric. The handbook describes the metric as quantifiable goals based on expected outputs for an organization. Additionally, a good metric must be specific and measurable. A system of metrics can be used to determine measure performance, as defined in the handbook. This assisted in the creation of the metrics used in the model framework.

Department of Defense. Defense Threat Reduction Agency. *Foreign Consequence Management: Legal Desk book*, 2007.
The book summarizes the sources of FCM within the USG. It displays the allocation of the agencies within the government such as DTRA and CMAP. As a result of the multitude of FCM agencies, it demonstrates the level of coordination in order to successfully respond to an emergency. The book, also, defines the FCM and the role that USG has within assisting a foreign nation. The communication and coordination for an FCM is given.

Gortney, William E. Office of the Chairman of the Joint Chiefs of Staff. *Chemical, Biological, Radiological, and Nuclear Consequence Management.* 21 June 2012.
The doctrine gives a standard for CBRNE CM within the USG. It encompasses both consequence management responses for CBRNE events within the United States and within PNs. The doctrine also establishes DTRA as the leading agency in charge of CBRNE FCM within the DoD. In order to mitigate the damages from possible CBRNE events, the procedures are designed for agencies such as DTRA and the Department of Homeland Security (DoS). The doctrine also demonstrates that extensive coordination is needed due to the numerous agencies within the USG.

Hubbard, Douglas W. *How to Measure Anything: Finding the Value of "intangibles" in Business.* Hoboken, NJ: John Wiley & Sons, 2007.
Douglas Hubbard writes how a company or an organization will be able to measure anything. He explains that "intangibles" are defined as things that are not measurable but argues that everything is measurable. The book assisted in the metric development and framework approach by reassuring that the metrics developed have to actually measure what DTRA desires within a PN CM.

Meyer, Marshall W. *Rethinking Performance Measurement: Beyond the Balanced Scorecard.* Cambridge, UK: Cambridge UP, 2002.
Through the analysis of multiple business firms and their subsequent failures, Meyer was able to determine a key factor was the lack of measuring performance. This article illustrates the importance of performance measurement. Also, it explains that the metrics should be attainable and designed to measure the desired performance. The information from Meyer assisted in designing metrics that were attainable and reasonable in accordance with the information gathered.

Moroney, Jennifer D. P. *Building Partner Capabilities for Coalition Operations.* Rand Corporation, 2007.
The article establishes the definitions of both capabilities and capacities and explains how they are essential in CMAP's purpose within the DoD and USG. Capabilities are defined as the country's ability to perform a function while capacity measures the country's capabilities (mobilization, availability, and sustainment). By building these two within a PN, CMAP is able to assist the USG in creating a stronger working atmosphere with PNs and establish greater national security. These two were established as overarching objectives within the qualitative value hierarchy.

National Research Council Staff. *Industrial Environmental Performance Metrics: Challenges and Opportunities.* Washington, DC: National Academy, 1999.
The research studied the multiple industries within the USG and the environmental impact that they had. The importance that this research served was their metric development and how they had approached the problem. Mirroring their metric development process, the metrics for the CMAP model was designed to capture the stakeholder wants, needs, and desires along with the organization's overall functions and objectives.

Office of the Secretary of Defense. Office of the Director of Administration and Management. *Organization of the Department of Defense,* 2008. http://odam.defense.gov/omp/Library/DoD Organizational Charts/DoD Organization March 2012. pdf.
This chart displays how the DoD is organized and where DTRA is located within the DoD system. Located under the Defense Agencies category, DTRA is also identified as a Combat Support Agency.
Parnell, Gregory S., Patrick J. Driscoll, and Dale L. Henderson. *Decision Making in Systems Engineering and Management.* Second Edition. New York: John Wiley and Sons, 2010.

This textbook defines the methodology that this project used to design the system. It establishes and explains the SDP that guided the system into completion. Specifically, the Problem Definition phase, Solution Design phase, and Decision Making phase were the ones utilized in the creation of the model. The last phase, Solution Implementation, was not used intricately used in the research because DTRA will be utilizing and adapting the model for better future applications.

Prins, Robert. *CMAP 101 PowerPoint Brief: June 2012 Mission Statement.*
The powerpoint presentation establishes the purpose and goals of CMAP. The brief also displayed their methodology and strategy that they used to reach their goals. This presentation also addresses the current shortcomings of CMAP and their consequence management program. These problems were identified as no ability to track progression over time. Through analysis of the brief, the project was created to help CMAP obtain the goals that they established and create a framework that solved the current problems that they faced.

Taylor, Scott R., Amy M. Rowe, and Brian M. Lewis. Center for Counter Proliferation Research National Defense University. *Consequence Management in Need of a Timeout.* 51st Communications Squadron. Washington, D.C.: Summer 1999. http://www.dtic.mil/cgi-bin/GetTRDoc?Location=U2&doc=GetTRDoc.pdf&AD=ADA426663.
This article explains the concerns that consequence management assesses. One primary concern is analyzing the PN's ability to plan and execute an incident response through the coordination and organized efforts of multiple agencies. Both of these abilities and execution are measured in the model through quantifiable metrics.

This Page Intentionally Left Blank

Appendix B
Acronyms

CBRNE	chemical, biological, radiation, nuclear, and high explosives
CMAP	Consequence Management Assistance Program
COCOM	Combatant Command
DTRA	Defense Threat Reduction Agency
DoD	Department of Defense
DoS	Department of State
FCM	Foreign Consequence Management
MODA	multi objective decision analysis
PN	partner nation
SDP	systems design process
USG	United States Government
USSTRATCOM	United States Strategic Command
USJFCOM	United States Joint Forces Command
WMD	weapons of mass destruction

This Page Intentionally Left Blank

Appendix C
Stakeholder Interviews

C.1 Interview 1 (Ft. Belvoir, VA on 11 September 2012)
Interviewee List:
- COL Clark Heidelbaugh (Chief, Consequence Management Division)
- Mr. Ben Cacioppo (Deputy Chief, Strategic Engagement Branch)
- CWO4 Terry Carden (Strategic Engagement Branch)
- LTC Robert D. Prins
- Strategic Engagement Branch Support Staff (Mr. David Leffler, Ms. Amanda Lloyd, Mr. Dale Bain)
- Consequence Management Division Support Staff (Mr. Keith McCollough)
- Building Partner Capacity Department Support Staff (Mr. Mike Bruce, Mr. Sean Remly)

Initial Stakeholder Meeting Results
1. Biggest problem is data management and availability
   a. Extract meanings from words
   b. To constrict the user or not to constrict
   c. NATO vs. US Standards
   d. Western Mindset vs. Eastern Mindset
   e. Narrowing the scope of the project
2. Tool for CMAP to impact foreign country and their capacity
   a. How specific cities respond to an event (Response)
   b. NYC = disaster response (#1 response program)
3. No one has been able to do it in the past
   a. Database has only been in effect in the last 7 years
   b. Budget cuts and constraints
   c. Current database cannot track progress
4. People, Training, Equipment-3 main things to track
5. CMAP
   a. Finds out what Consequence Management means to other nations
   b. What does a successful response look like at every level and for every country
   c. See CMAPs progress over the past year-from start to now
6. Metrics
   a. Programmatic-See handout
   b. Country-Measures across time
   c. Execution-Department of Homeland Security
   d. Mesh b and c together
7. Overview (Diagram)
   a. How do we measure progress? – By using metric analysis
   b. Why? – To establish standards for countries
   c. Question? – Sustainable over time? Achievable? Feasible? Justifiable? Relatable?
8. Categorizing Countries
   a. Economic, geographical, other capabilities
   b. Some countries will require different approaches
      i. Some responders are under civilian
      ii. Others are under military

C.2 Interview 2 (Teleconference on 19 September 2012)

Interviewee:

- LTC Robert D. Prins
- Mr. Mark Melanson

New Questions and Responses from LTC Rob Prins

1. What stakeholders other than DTRA might there be? (Who will be some of our other users?)
   At this time the primary stakeholders are DTRA CMAP. DTRA CMAP not only engages with U.S. Government Interagency but also with other members of the Department of Defense (primarily the Geographic Combatant Commanders and their different components) in addition to Partner Nations with the respective U.S. Embassies.

2. Can we please get a list of all of the stakeholders we met with last week?
   COL Clark Heidelbaugh (Chief, Consequence Management Division); Mr. Ben Cacioppo (Deputy Chief, Strategic Engagement Branch); CWO4 Terry Carden (Strategic Engagement Branch); Strategic Engagement Branch Support Staff (Mr. David Leffler, Ms. Amanda Lloyd, Mr. Dale Bain); Consequence Management Division Support Staff (Mr. Keith McCollough); Building Partner Capacity Department Support Staff (Mr. Mike Bruce, Mr. Sean Remly)

3. Do you have any suggestions on how we can narrow the scope of the project? Right now we are concerned that we may have too broad of a focus, and we would like to be able to narrow it down before we continue going through our stakeholder analysis. At this time, I would begin by understanding the problem. I would also really start to understand the mechanisms by which you are going to build a statistical framework that is able to perform quantitative analysis with qualitative metrics. This is incredibly important to me. Your ability to also assist me in developing metrics is a secondary effort. The framework must be capable of allowing me to input metrics, their description, and their methods (yes/no, 1-10, etc.). I am going to be using your framework to look across three different levels; programmatic, individual country, and then individual engagement.
   - Can you explain more about the distinction between these three levels?
     Different metrics are used for each level. The framework should be able to accept all of these levels of metrics.
   Programmatic is the strategic level of metrics.
   Individual country is DTRA's interaction and how they progress over 1-3 years.
   Individual/unique engagement is the 1 year engagement. Each engagement is going to going to be measuring a submission area → you will need to pick and choose which ones you will measure.
   - What is your suggestion on selection criteria for which ones you will measure?
     Depends on the **type of engagement** and who you will be interacting with. The framework must be broad enough to accept this and not limiting that you can't take a metric out later on. Some performance measures are already unique to the type of engagement.

4. At the tail end of the meeting on Tuesday you talked about the role of the State Department and the legal issues that you have to deal with. Can you further define the role of DTRA and the State Department in dealing with CMAP and how that is important to our problem? Funny you ask, I just had a meeting with the Department of State Foreign Consequence Management (FCM) personnel today. State Department (FCM) is the U.S. Government Lead Agent for foreign consequence management. CMAP therefore has to fully work with State to ensure not transparency and openness between our work but also to make sure that efforts are coordinated. When working with foreign countries, CMAP has Title 10 authority meaning that we can only primarily work with other militaries. However, State has Title 22 which allows them to work with foreign civilian agencies. Consequence management requires the meshing of response forces

(military plus civilian) therefore CMAP's "civilian partner" must logically be Department of State. There are other entities of course but this is a good starting point.

Teleconference Question and Answers

1. Who collects all of the data for DTRA? Data for engagements are collected by individuals from the Strategic Engagement Branch (and support staff) that engage directly with the Partner Nations. For example, I am going to the Philippines next week to conduct a seminar with representatives from the Filipino Armed Forces. Data for countries is going to be mixture of data collected by the engagement leads (branch personnel) and information input from the Combatant Command staffs. Data for the programmatic is going to come from interactions with all our stakeholders.
   - What training do the branch personnel receive? Is there any type of calibration?
   They receive baseline training for collecting data. Their broad scope of knowledge will be narrowed down to the type of position you have. People in DTRA branch receive training on how FEMA operates. Learn about national response framework, etc. Framework should provide a way to measure the metrics but also make recommendations on how to collect and store the data (through an iPad, etc).

2. Where and how is this data stored? Currently we have no real strong data storage mechanism other that basic saving into a computer shared drive. You have hit yet another nail on the head in that eventually the data must be in a format that is "meta-data" searchable that will eventually input directly into the framework which you are working on. Clear as mud?

3. Do you have an organizational diagram that shows where DTRA and CMAP fall into the bigger picture? Do you mean within DOD? DTRA is a Department of Defense Agency. This a good question that if you mean within DOD then we will get you something. Bring this up in the telecom and directly ask...I will then ask Mr. Leffler to help get you this. Good question because as an LT you will need to understand who all your "friendlies" are and how they are capable of supporting the mission not to mention how your mission supports them.
   - DoS FCM → How difficult is it to work with them and what system do they use? How long have they been around?
   By law, DoS is the lead agent for consequence management. They have been doing it for a long time. They are easy to work with. The challenge is that they are not as big as DoD, so they are given a lot of authority with not many people. DoD has the people and DoS has the authority. We meet with them regularly.
   - Do we have a way to tie their system into ours?
   They do not have a system, but they have a program with a few people that work with it. There is nothing we will really be able to take from them to help us. Whatever we come up with, there is a good chance they will use it too.

4. How does the system work? (From collecting the data in the field to analyzing it in DTRA) Slowly. Crudely. Our program is still relatively new (less than a year old) so we are still working on figuring things out. Your questions help me identify gaps that may exist so that I can help address them for my boss (Mr. Darrin Flick).
   - What is the exact process used? Where does the data go from data collector to DTRA?
   It is your job to give us a recommendation on how to do it. Give us an unbiased perspective on our concerns for this.
   - How in depth do you want us to get? Are we focusing on the framework or are we going further?
   Be careful not to do mission creep. Be careful we don't get too in-depth. If time permits and the framework is complete, take some extra time to pursue it. Otherwise focus on the framework. GIVE RECOMMENDATIONS – you don't have to necessarily follow through with everything (maybe use models).

C.3 Interview 2 Follow-up (E-mail on 1 October 2012)

Interviewee:

* Mr. David Leffler

1. We would like further clarification on the roles of all the stakeholders within DTRA. For example what is the role of the Strategic Branch Support Staff?
We would like to know their areas of expertise within CMAP so that we can ask them specific questions about their field as those questions come up.
Is it alright to contact these stakeholders on an individual level, and if so can we have their email addresses?
Currently we have email addresses for Mr. Bain, Ms. Lloyd, Mr. Melanson, Mr. Cacioppo, Mr. Flick, and COL Heidelbaugh.

Below is an organizational chart depicting the positions and personnel in CMAP (outlined in blue) and the Division and Branch leadership under whom the program falls.

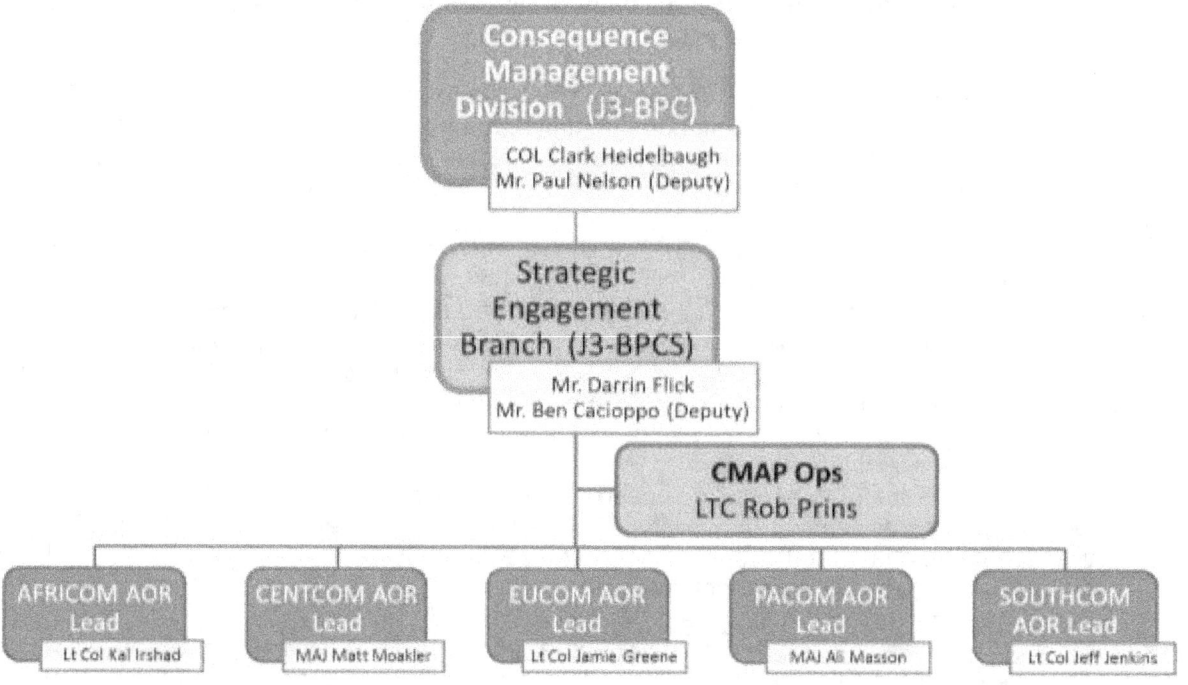

Additional contact info:

* LTC Rob Prins (Medical; nuclear physics): robert.prins@dtra.mil
  * Mr. Dave Leffler [contract support to LTC Prins]: david.leffler@cubic.com / david.leffler_contractor@dtra.mil
* Lt Col Kal Irshad (Medical): khalid.irshad@dtra.mil
  * Ms. Jessica Olcott [contract support to Lt Col Irshad]: jessica.olcott@cubic.com / jessica.olcott_contractor@dtra.mil
* MAJ Matt Moakler (CBRN/Engineer): matthew.moakler@dtra.mil
* Lt Col Jamie Greene (EOD): james.greene@dtra.mil
  * Ms. Olcott [contract support to Lt Col Greene]
* MAJ Ali Masson (CBRN): alicia.masson@dtra.mil
  * Ms. Nancy Blanford [contract support to MAJ Masson]: nancy.blanford@cubic.com / nancy.blanford_contractor@dtra.mil

- Lt Col Jeff Jenkins (____): jeffrey.jenkins@dtra.mil
    - Mr. Ricardo Agudelo [contract support to Lt Col Jenkins]: ricardo.agudelo@cubic.com / ricardo.agudelo_contractor@dtra.mil

2. What does the baseline training for branch personnel that collect data consist of?
And is it possible for us to get a copy of that training?
We know it is still very new but are trying to understand the process as it is now as best we can.

There is currently no codified or official "data collection" process and, as such, there is no specific training regimen associated with data collection. The Measures of Effectiveness (MOEs) that were recently developed by Mr. Bain and Ms. Lloyd and approved by Mr. Cacioppo will serve as guides for data collection and will hopefully lead to the establishment of a standardized collection and analysis process across CMAP and all COCOM AORs

3. Would you be willing to give us a point of contact for the Department of State? It is important that we get their perspective as well to ensure coverage of all the stakeholders. We will give them a brief introduction to our problem and ask a few questions to gain a holistic view of the whole system.

The POC CMAP through whom CMAP has been coordinating with DOS is Mr. Corey Hamilton. LTC Prins will confirm Mr. Hamilton's availability to assist and make the introduction over e-mail.

4. Initial questions we came up with regarding the Department of State's role are:
What is the DoS role in the three levels regarding programmatic, individual country, and individual engagement?

CMAP currently operates in a Title 10 capacity (i.e., mil-to-mil) and cannot engage directly with civilians, including non-military law enforcement and other incident responders. DOS, on the other hand, operates according to Title 22 which grants the ability to engage with civilians though not directly with military forces. In a sense, CMAP and DOS are inverses of each other in terms of their legal limitations/permissions for engaging with personnel of foreign nations. Because CBRN incident response is often not purely a military effort and incorporates civilian capabilities and personnel, the CMAP-DOS partnership is sometimes necessary in order to engage with the complete span of response capabilities of a Partner Nation rather than solely its civilian or military components.
Additionally, DOS supports the CMAP mission by assisting DTRA to build relationships with Partner Nations through diplomatic channels and other civilian relationships which the military (i.e., DTRA) typically cannot access.

What are the top three concerns that the DoS has with consequence management when it relates to metrics?

1. No metrics for CM currently exist so each department/agency involved with CM (DOS, DoD, USAID, DOE, etc.) uses its own guidelines and measurements to determine success rather than coordinating with each other to streamline efforts and present a more unified effort to a given Host Nation/Partner Nation.

General
1. Even with the excel breakdown of the focus areas, we still don't have a clear understanding of what each of the metrics mean.

a. What is the current procedure for measuring all of these metrics? There is currently no official procedure for measurement for a couple reasons: CMAP is completing its first year of operations and the program is still in the "Planning" phase during which the groundwork for future execution events (i.e., the opportunities for data collection) is developed; additionally, the current metrics have only recently been approved by Mr. Cacioppo/Mr. Flick and have not yet been put into use. CMAP personnel at events so far have taken individual notes throughout engagement events, recording the dialogues and questions, to begin assembling a general profile on each Partner Nation's capabilities as a foundation on which to add subsequent details as the engagement process continues. The information aggregated from these notes is the basis for establishing the baseline we will use to judge progress later.

b. Are we supposed to focus on a general method for you to analyze your own metrics so you can add them to the framework over time? Or do you want us to focus on developing the most important focus areas that we believe each country should have? Closer to the former: we would like you to work to determine how to measure subjective/qualitative metrics objectively/quantitatively. This involves the persistent question in statistics of how to measure details that are indefinite. For example, the question "Does country X have plans to respond to incident type Y?" could be answered "yes/no", but within that binary answer is implicitly a question of degree (i.e., "To what extent is the answer 'yes/no'?").

c. Should the framework contain two different types of metrics? (One for incident response readiness and one for post-incident) We are not committed to one way or the other, though the two-set approach will likely be more manageable for your analysis and effective in our execution. That being said, if you determine a way to use one set of metrics efficiently (e.g., "Capability X is sufficient for ABC" is measured once for readiness and separately for post-incident response), then we welcome your thoughts about that as well.

2. Which level do you think DTRA is most concerned about? (Do you think the focus is on measuring the programmatic, country, or individual level?) The focus of CMAP is to assist in building Partner Nations' response capacities at the national level. Sometimes this will translate to engaging at the tactical or operational level, though we are not concerned with the abilities of individual personnel or units, per se; we are interested in the given country's development of its overall response capabilities.

Functional Flow
1. How do you determine where to go and when to go there? Does someone from DoS or DoD give you directives for where to travel/which countries we need information on? As a COCOM support agency, DTRA relies heavily on the stated regional needs and priorities of each COCOM; CMAP operates in this way, making most programmatic and planning decisions based on coordination with counterparts at each COCOM. Sometimes, however, some engagement decisions are made based on diplomatic priorities as DOS, not DoD, would be the lead agency in the event of a CBRN incident that required foreign consequence management operations. Additionally, available funding is always a consideration, as is a Partner Nation's availability or interest. Determining which PNs to engage and when to do so is more an art than a science. The engagement COAs are presented by each CMAP COCOM AOR lead to Mr. Flick (or Mr. Cacioppo in Mr. Flick's absence) and/or COL Heidelbaugh for approval.

2. What other agencies do you share your findings with? Currently we work with DOS Foreign Consequence Management (FCM) program and the National Guard State Partnership Programs (SPPs). The NG of most states have each partnered with a foreign nation for the sake of cross-training, education, exchanged programs, relationship-building, etc. The NG units often serve to introduce the CMAP program to given Partner Nations and to facilitate CMAP engagement event planning and coordination.

Functional Hierarchy

1. Levels of metrics
   a. When we were going through the different focus areas, we tried to redefine what "Programmatic, Country, and Individual" meant to us. This is our basic understanding: Programmatic – Plans, procedures, and long term goals for an organization; Country – Operational goals and procedures that focus on the 2-5 year time frame; Individual – the current readiness state of the programs (how they would respond within one year of an incident). Is this basic understanding correct? For the most part, yes, your understanding is correct. The only modification is that we would consider what you have within "Individual" to fall under "Country" in addition to what you already have under the "Country" heading; all of those considerations affect the Partner Nation at the country-wide level, i.e., whether the country as a whole would be able to respond to an incident. We define "Individual" as the response capacity at the level of the response personnel, themselves. Sometimes individual capacity could have Country- or Programmatic-level consequences (similar to the concept of the "strategic corporal"), which is why we do sometimes engage PNs at the tactical-level, such as in the AFRICOM AOR.

Notes

1. As we were going through the metrics, we noticed that each of the focus areas could fit into all three of the levels. We tried to put them into the level that we felt it would be actually measured in.
   a. This made us realize that the programmatic (or strategic) goals were the most important part of every single focus area. Without an overall organization goal or vision, it's impossible to develop the nitty-gritty individual response metrics.
   b. The programmatic level can be measured *using* the other two levels. If we can measure the metrics in the individual and country levels, we may be able to assess the overall status of the programmatic level.
2. This is how we see the framework working:
   a. DTRA and country agree on a strategic goal (depends on their capabilities).
   b. Data collector measures individual metrics (current state of readiness...how ready the country is within one year for an incident).
   c. Data collector measures country metrics (operational state of readiness... the way ahead to enhance readiness or what happens after the initial response in 2-5 year range).
   d. Using these two levels, the programmatic level can be assessed by DTRA.

C.4 Interview 3 (E-mail on 5 November 2012)

Interviewee:
- LTC Robert D. Prins

Observations and Recommendations
- There is a disconnect between all of the sources of metrics.
  - ➢ A functional hierarchy will combine the CMAP sub-mission areas, the commonalties, and end states.
  - ➢ The metrics should fit into the MOEs and the MOEs should fit into the end states.

- Give some recommendations on how data should be collected and the entire system should work.
  - ➢ The data collectors should go through calibrated training.
  - ➢ Metrics can have a number scale (ex. 1-5), and word pictures should be associated with every number on the scale.
  - ➢ There are many different options for data storage (Redi, Access).

- Adding and deleting metrics from the framework for each engagement limits your ability to compare countries and measure them over time.
  - ➢ Use the same framework for every country.
  - ➢ In order to create a framework that can be used every time, the metrics must be filtered so that we only use the ones that can be measured anytime and anywhere.

- We have to be sure that the metrics measure the things they are actually supposed to (infrastructure, organization, personnel, and equipment).

- Outside constraints, DoS, and other agencies will be considered.
  - ➢ While FCM and CMAP work together well when it is necessary, they do not really share ideas or work together throughout the whole process.
  - ➢ Collaboration continues to exist between FCM and CMAP so that they are not doing two parallel assessments.

The Way Ahead
- Build a framework using Microsoft excel.
- Create the finalized functional hierarchy with the most important value measures.
- Stakeholders provide feedback on importance of value measures to create a swing weight matrix.
- Create a system for measuring every value measure (If the scale is from 1-5, a word picture should be associated with each number so measurement can be standardized).

Appendix D
Findings, Conclusions, and Recommendations Table

Findings	Conclusions	Recommendation
DTRA's biggest problem is data management and availability. There is no set procedural way to collect or store data. Any new system is starting from scratch.	Stakeholders want a recommendation on how the data should be collected (not necessarily very detailed). They also want a recommendation for how the entire system should work (from data collection to analysis). There is no way to compare countries and it limits measuring them over time.	Take into account the need for metrics to reflect commonalities and end states, quantitative assessment, and measurable value measures across all countries, in a simplistic framework. How this data is collected, assessed, and used should be a primary focus. A functional hierarchy will combine the CMAP submission areas, the commonalties, and end states. Outside constraints, DoS, and other agencies will be considered.
Data comes from a mixture of input from engagement leads (branch representatives) and input from the Combatant Command staffs. Data collectors go to countries and ask questions to assemble a general profile of each partner nation. This information establishes the baseline they will use to measure progress later. Metrics are added and deleted according to the country that the stakeholder is analyzing. Different people go every time and their data collection is not standardized or calibrated.		
Framework should be **broad** and **simple.** It should be capable of inputting metrics, a description of each metric, and the methods to measure them (yes/no, scale).	Extracting meaning from all of the current metrics and systems will be difficult. The metrics must be filtered for the most important ones that are value-focused – choose ones that can be measured anytime and anywhere. The metrics should assess the things they are supposed to (organization, infrastructure, and personnel).	
The framework used will depend on the type of engagement that is taking place (will need to be adjusted).		
Framework should include three levels of metrics: Strategic, operational, and tactical. There are three main areas data needs to be collected for: people, training, and equipment.		
Metrics should focus on quantitative measures and avoid qualitative. They should be justifiable, sustainable, feasible, and achievable. They should also have longevity.		
Metrics are not organized. There are too many because they are too specific.		
Consequence Management is for 96 hours after an event (CBRNE events mainly).	Establish the different things that are measured after a CBRNE disaster.	
This system will be a tool for CMAP to impact a partner nation's response abilities.	The different capabilities of countries will be a main consideration. The framework should be broad and flexible enough to assess any country over an undefined period of time.	
Each country will have to be evaluated separately because they all have different response capabilities (affected by infrastructure, economy, etc). A successful response will be different for each country. Also consider that countries have different approaches (some of their programs will be under civilian and some military).		
FCM is a very small group of people that is the U.S. Government Lead Agent for FCM. CMAP must work closely and transparently with them so that all of their efforts are coordinated.	CMAP and the FCM (DoS) must work very closely together because neither can operate independently. Any coordination between CMAP and foreign civilian agencies needs to occur, it will need to go through the FCM.	
There is no coordination between CMAP and DoS, or any other agency, in measuring metrics or streamlining effort (there is no unified effort).		
CMAP has Title 10 authority, meaning they can only primarily work with foreign militaries. The Department of State has Title 22 which allows them to work with foreign civilian agencies.		

There are three different ways for assessing countries: 1) Goal #2 Partner Nation from chart 2) CMAP Mission Areas from functional hierarchy 3) Commonalities between End states from chart.	There are no connections between the sources of metrics and we will need to reorganize them in order to create a roll up of all of the metrics. The metrics should fit into the MOEs and the MOEs should fit into the end states.	
Possible end states: Capacity-the intang ble means for response (i.e. leadership, organization, etc.) Capabilities- tangible and physical (i.e. training, exercise, execution.	Take into consideration these two end states in the development of the functional hierarchy, and possibly be able to associate quantitative values with each in order to evaluate countries.	

Appendix E
Metric Breakdown

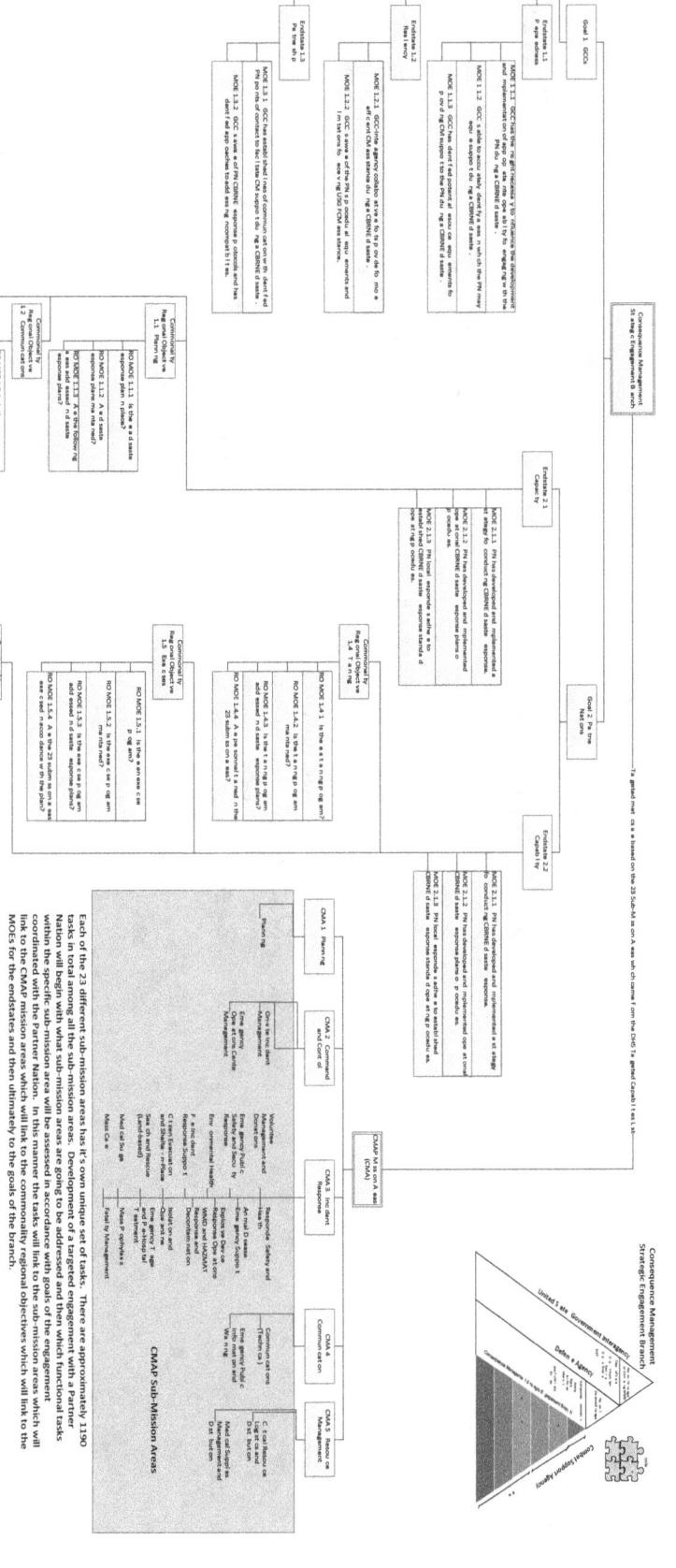

This Page Intentionally Left Blank

Appendix F
Stakeholder Program Focus Areas

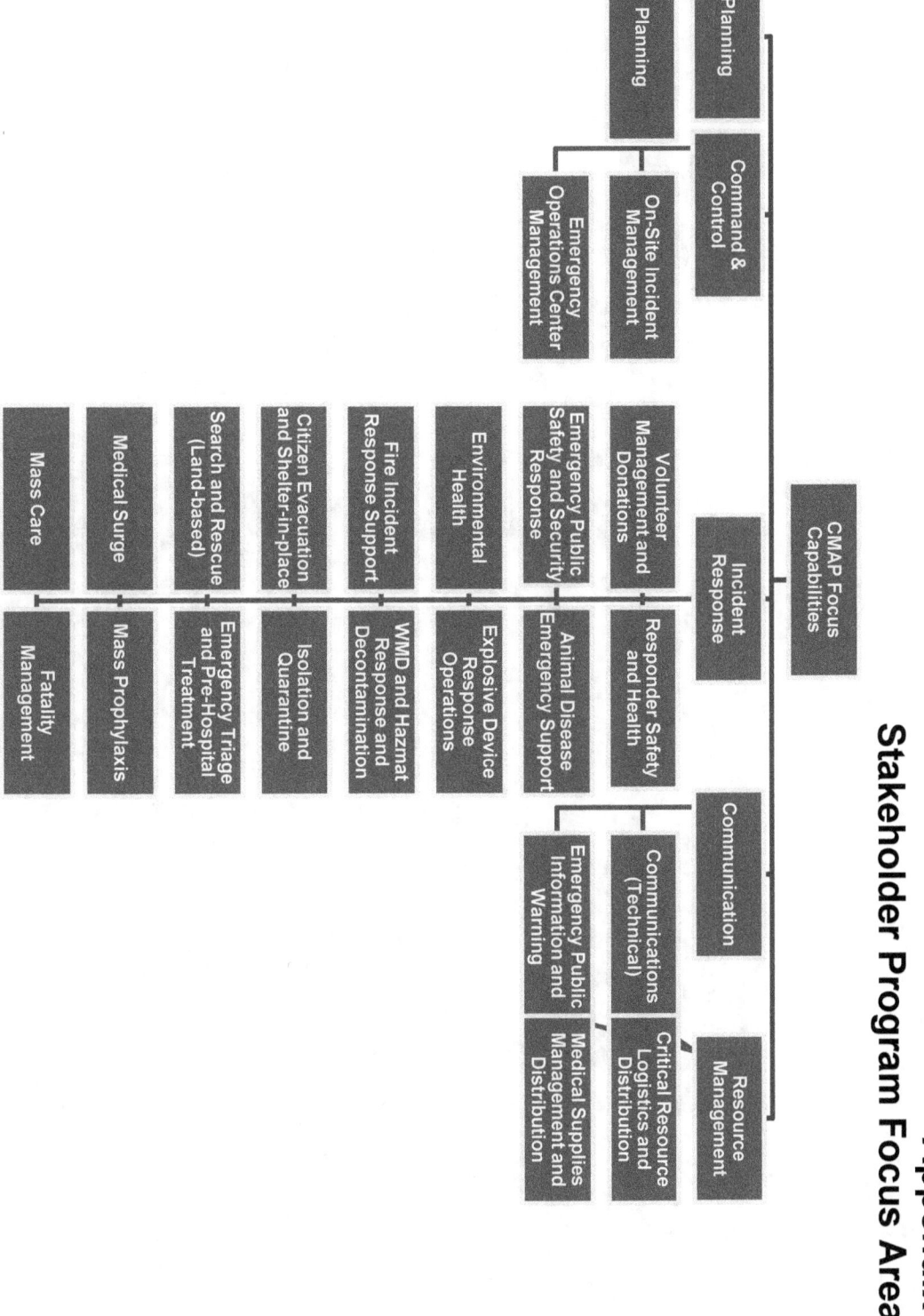

This Page Intentionally Left Blank

Appendix G
Stakeholder Activities Breakdown

	Sub-Mission Area	Activities
Planning	1. Planning	Conduct Strategic Planning
		Develop/Revise Operational Plans
Command and Control	2. On-Site Incident Management	Direct On-Site Incident Management
		Implement On-Site Incident Management
		Establish Full On-Site Incident Command
		Conduct Resource Management
		Develop Incident Action Plan (IAP)
		Execute Plan
		Demobilize On-Site Incident Management
	3. Emergency Operations Center Management	Direct Emergency Operation Center's Tactical Operations
		Activate EOC/MACC/IOF
		Information Consolidation and Issue Processing
		Coordinate Response
		Demobilize Emergency Operations Center Management
Incident Response	4. Volunteer Management and Donations	Coordinate Volunteer Management Operations and the Establishment of Warehouses and Materials Handling Equipment
		Activate Volunteer Management and Donations Emergency Plan
		Organize Volunteers and Assign them to Disaster Relief Efforts
		Collect and Manage Material Donations
		Collect and Manage Cash Donations
		Distribution of Donations
	5. Emergency Public Safety and Security Response	Command and Control Public Safety and Security Response Operations
		Activate Public Safety and Security Response
		Assess the Incident Scene and Secure the Area
		Control Traffic, Crowd, and Scene
		Conduct Law Enforcement Operations
		Manage Criminal Justice Population
	6. Environmental Health	Direct Environmental Health Operations (Command and Control)
		Activate Environmental Health
		Ensure Safety of Portable Water Supplies
		Ensure Safety of Food Supplies
		Ensure Safety of Wastewater Management
		Provide Vector Surveillance
		Ensure Safety of Building Environments
		Ensure Safety of Outdoor Environments
		Provide Environmental Health Support to Mass Care Response
		Provide Environmental Health Support to Solid Waste/Debris Removal
	7. Fire Incident Response Support	Activate Fire Incident Response Support
		Direct Fire Incident Response Support Tactical Operations
		Search Scene and Rescue

		Assess, Characterize, Conduct Operations, Forensics
	8. Citizen Evacuation and Shelter-in-place	Direct Evacuation and/or In-Place Protection Tactical Operations
		Activate Evacuation and/or In-Place Protection
		Implement Evacuation Orders for General Population
		Collect and Evacuate Population Requiring Assistance
		Operate Evacuation Staging/Reception Area
		Manage Incoming Evacuees
		Implement In-Place Protection Procedures
		Assist Re-Entry
	9. Search and Rescue (Land-based)	Direct Search & Rescue Tactical Operations
		Activate Search & Rescue
		Conduct Search and Rescue Reconnaissance
		Search and Extricate
		Provide Medical Treatment
	10. Medical Surge	Direct Medical Surge Tactical Operations
		Activate Medical Surge
		Implement Surge Patient Transfer Procedures
		Implement Surge Staffing Procedures
		Receive and Treat Surge Casualties
	11. Mass Care	Direct Mass Care Operations
		Activate Mass Care
		Establish Shelter Operations (includes closure)
		Shelter General Population
		Shelter Companion Animals
		Establish Feeding Operations
		Prepare and Distribute Food
		Establish Bulk Distribution Operations
		Conduct Bulk Distribution Operations
	12. Responder Safety and Health	Direct Responder Safety and Health Tactical Operations
		Activate Responder Safety and Health
		Identify Safety/PPE Needs and Distribute PPE
		Ongoing Monitoring of Responder Safety and Health
	13. Animal Disease Emergency Support	Direct Animal Disease Emergency Support Tactical Operations
		Conduct Animal Health Epidemiological Investigation & Surveillance
		Implement Disease Containment Measures
		Conduct Euthanasia/Disposal
	14. Explosive Device Response Operations	Direct Explosive Device Response Operations
		Search and Assess Site
		Render Safe Onsite
		Conduct Recovery, Removal, and Transport Operations
	15. WMD and HAZMAT Response and Decontamination	Direct WMD and Hazardous Materials Response and Decontamination Tactical Operations
		Identify the Hazard
		Assess Hazard, Evaluate Risk, Conduct Rescue Operations
		Adjust Mitigation Strategies
		Decontaminate and Recover
	16. Isolation and	Direct Isolation and Quarantine Tactical Operations

		Activate Isolation and Quarantine
	Quarantine	Implement Travel Restrictions
	17. Emergency Triage and Pre-Hospital Treatment	Direct Triage and Pre-Hospital Treatment Tactical Operations
		Activate Triage and Pre-Hospital Treatment
		Triage
		Provide Treatment
		Transport
	18. Mass Prophylaxis	Direct Mass Prophylaxis Tactical Operations
		Activate Mass Prophylaxis Dispensing Operations
		Establish Points of Dispensing
		Conduct Triage for Symptoms
		Conduct Medical Screening
		Conduct Mass Dispensing
		Monitor Adverse Events
	19. Fatality Management	Direct Fatality Management Tactical Operations
		Activate Fatality Management Operations
		Conduct On-Scene Fatality Management Operations
		Conduct Morgue Operations
		Manage Ante mortem Data
		Conduct Victim Identification
		Conduct Final Disposition
Communication	20. Communications (Technical)	Alert and Dispatch
		Provide Incident Command/First Responder/First Receiver/Interoperable Communications
		Provide Emergency Operations Center Communications Support
	21. Emergency Public Information and Warning	Manage Emergency Public Information and Warnings
		Activate Emergency Public Information, Alert/Warning, and Notification Plans
		Establish Joint Information Center
		Conduct Joint Information Center Operations
		Issue Public Information, Alerts/Warnings, and Notifications
		Conduct Media Relations
		Provide Public Rumor Control
Resource Management	22. Critical Resource Logistics and Distribution	Direct Critical Resource Logistics and Distribution Operations
		Activate Critical Resource Logistics and Distribution
		Respond to Needs Assessment and Inventory
		Acquire Resources
		Transport, Track, and Manage Resources
		Maintain and Recover Resources
	23. Medical Supplies Management and Distribution	Direct Medical Supplies Management and Distribution Tactical Operations
		Activate Medical Supplies Management and Distribution
		Establish Security
		Repackage and Distribute
		Recover Medical Resources

This Page Intentionally Left Blank

Appendix H
Maximize Organization Objective

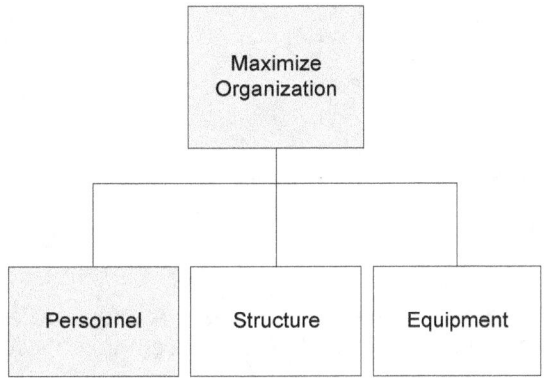

Personnel

Definition: Personnel are the body of persons employed by consequence management organizations.

0- None

1- Identify personnel requirements.
Identify gaps in requirements.

2- All personnel receive formal training (passed test).

3- Personnel placed into organizational structure.

4- Identify leadership positions, selected by experienced and qualified personnel.

5- Performance feedback and personnel evaluation. Structured personnel feedback mechanism to ensure the most qualified people are in the right positions.

Score	Values
0	0
1	25
2	50
3	67
4	85
5	100

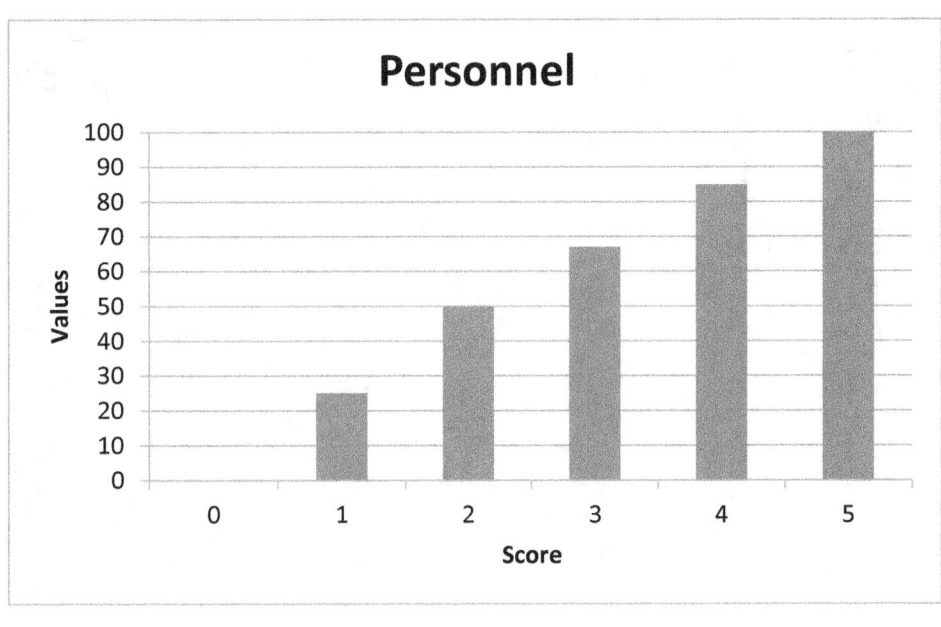

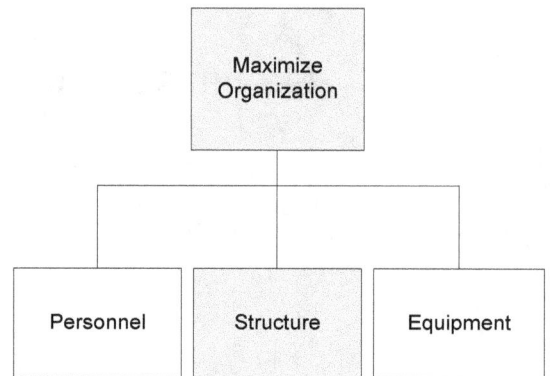

Structure

Definition: Structure is the arrangement of responsibilities, authorities, and relationships amongst the different organizations and people in order to collaborate to accomplish a common goal.

0- None

1- Identify type of organization (matrix, linear, hierarchical).

2- Established doctrine with defined roles and responsibilities.
Baseline management competencies are achieved.
> Long range calendar
> Top level organization structure
> Strategic vision
> Basic communications plan
> Strategic budgeting mechanism

3- Organization is populated by trained personnel.

4- Organization is evaluated by an outside agency.

5- Adjusts structure based on evaluations over time (continually growing).

Score	Values
0	0
1	25
2	58
3	78
4	92
5	100

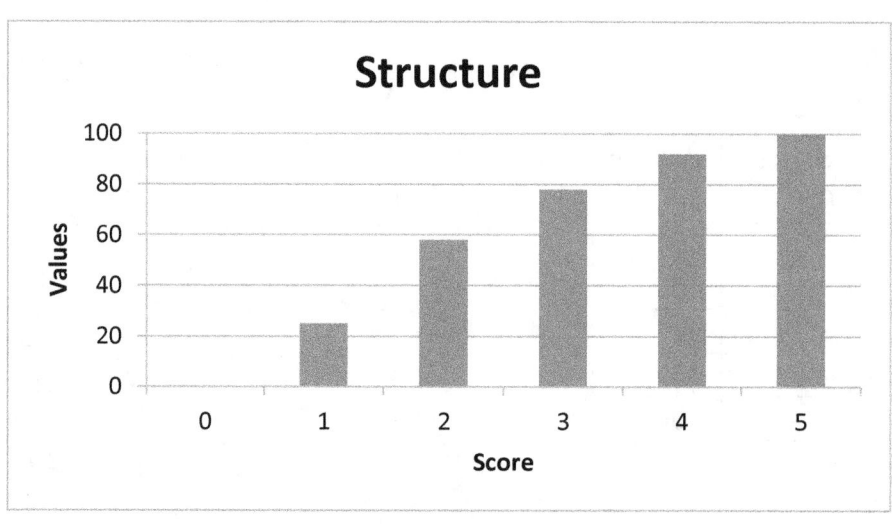

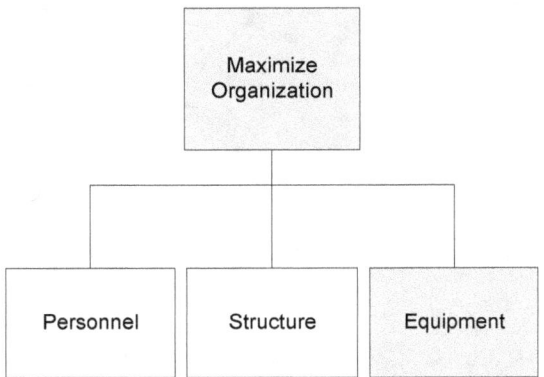

Equipment

Definition: Equipment is all of the necessary tools and systems needed in order to accomplish the organization's goals.

0- None

1- Established logistical system.

2- Identify needs of organization.

3- Personnel users are trained and training program is in place.

4- Available equipment inventoried and maintained.

5- Future needs plans in place for replacement and upgrading of equipment.

Score	Values
0	0
1	19
2	33
3	64
4	83
5	100

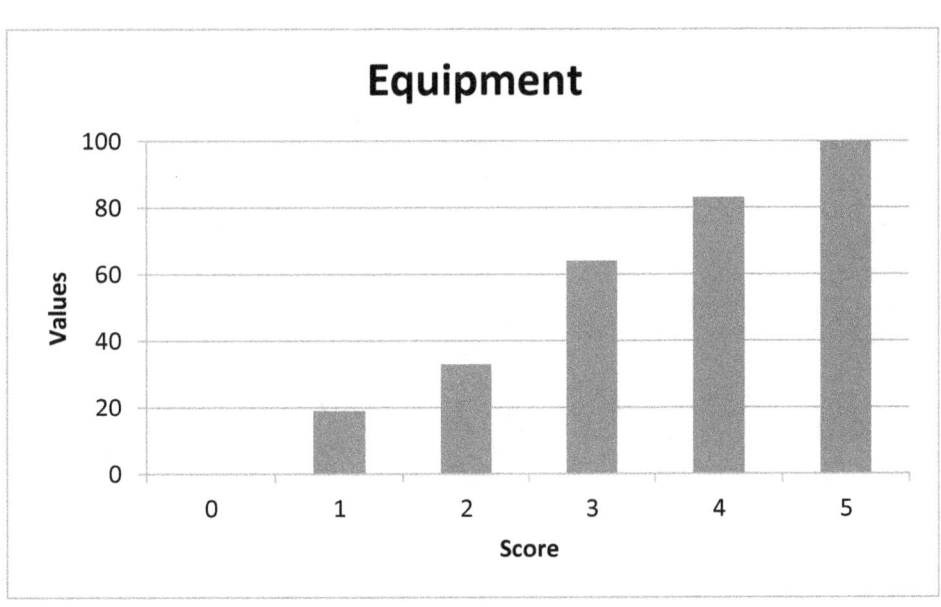

This Page Intentionally Left Blank

Appendix I
Optimize Planning Objective

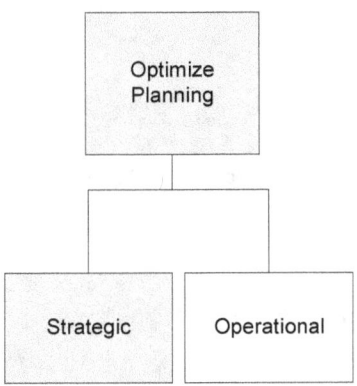

Strategic Planning

Definition: Planning that emphasizes operations for all possible emergencies.

0- None

1- Established doctrine (guidance, tactics, tasks, and procedures):
   Vision for emergency preparedness
   Emergency response execution

2- Established command and control structure for each emergency, with roles and responsibilities defined.

3- Plans/doctrine are easily accessible and understood by personnel.

4- All personnel formally trained.

5- Ability to monitor current operations in order to obtain feedback to reassess and improve current plans.

Score	Values
0	0
1	33
2	53
3	69
4	84
5	100

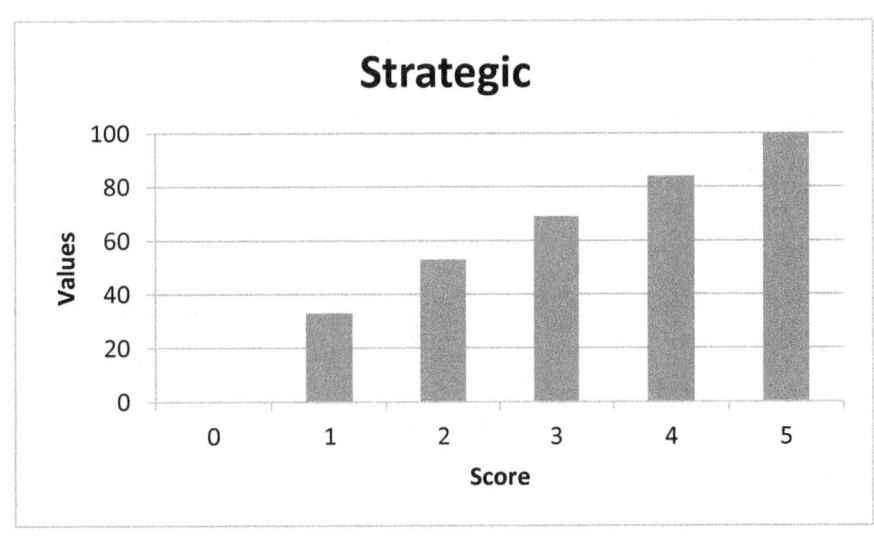

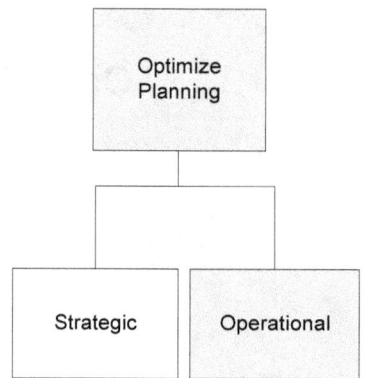

Operational Planning

Definition: Planning that emphasizes training and exercises.

0- None

1- Established doctrine (guidance, tactics, tasks, and procedures):
    Training calendar
    Training events

2- Established command and control structure, with roles and responsibilities defined.

3- Plans/doctrine are easily accessible and understood by personnel.

4- All personnel formally trained.

5- Ability to monitor current operations in order to obtain feedback to reassess and improve current plans.

Score	Values
0	0
1	37
2	58
3	73
4	90
5	100

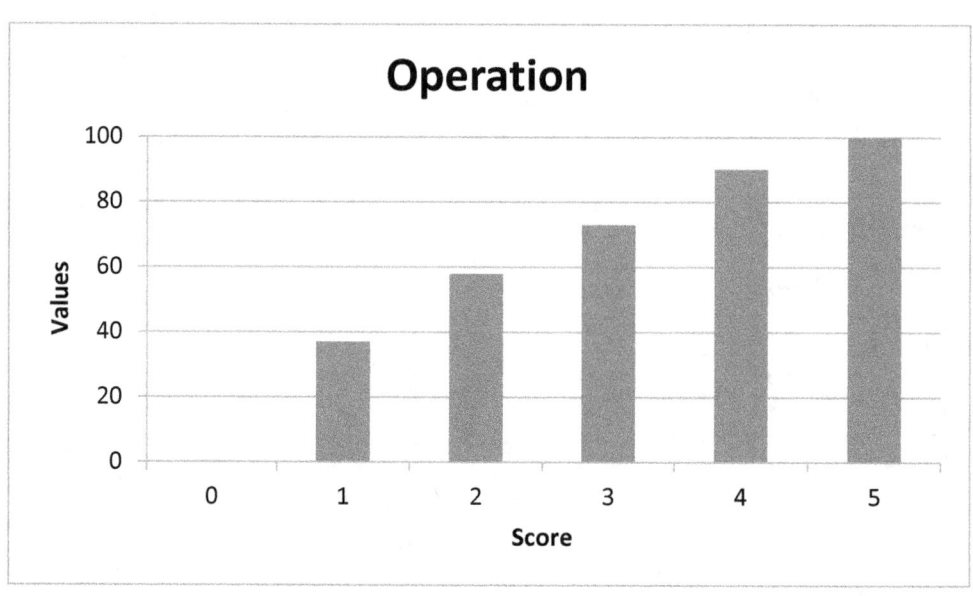

Appendix J
Maximize Communication Objective

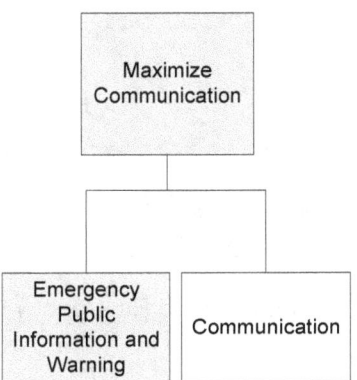

Emergency Public Information and Warning

Definition: Ability to issue public information, alerts/warnings, and notifications through an established joint information center (JIC), which measures the effectiveness of media relations and the ability to control the public message.

0- None

1- Established doctrine (guidance, tactics, tasks, and procedures):
    Establish emergency information and public warnings plan
    Manage emergency public information and warnings
    Issue public information, alerts/warnings, and notifications
    Conduct media relations
    Provide public rumor control

2- Established command and control structure, with roles and responsibilities defined.

3- Direct emergency JIC operations and warnings.
Plans/doctrine are easily accessible and understood by personnel.
Ability to execute plans is present.

4- Exercise and validate plans.
All personnel formally trained.

5- Ability to monitor current operations in order to obtain feedback to reassess and improve current doctrine and organization.

Score	Values
0	0
1	37
2	54
3	72
4	89
5	100

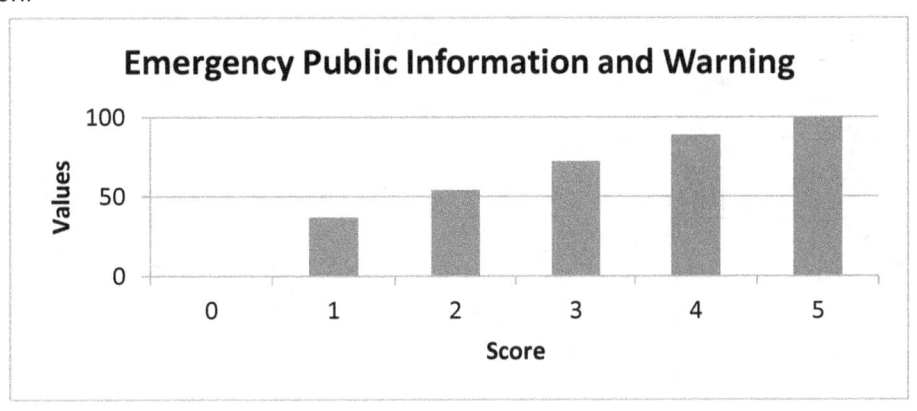

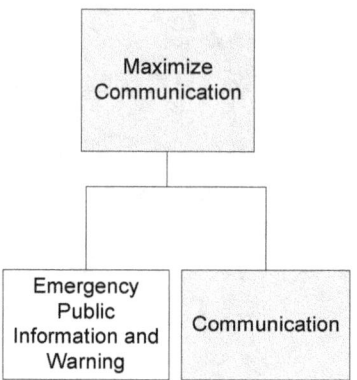

Communication

Definition: The three-way communication between the Emergency Operations Center (EOC), the incident command, and the first responders.

0- None

1- Established doctrine (guidance, tactics, tasks, and procedures):
    Establish communication operations plan
    Provide necessary equipment to facilitate communications
    Provide interoperable communications between:
        EOC
        Incident command
        First responder

2- Established command and control structure, with roles and responsibilities defined.

3- Direct communication operations.
    Plans/doctrine are easily accessible and understood by personnel.
    Ability to execute plans is present.

4- Exercise and validate plans.
    All personnel formally trained.

5- Ability to monitor current operations in order to obtain feedback to reassess and improve current doctrine and organization.

Score	Values
0	0
1	28
2	48
3	65
4	85
5	100

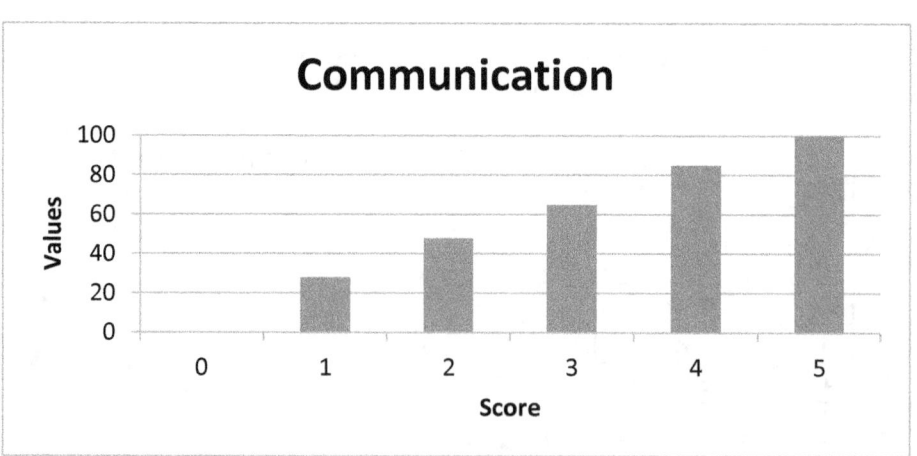

Appendix K
Maximize Command and Control Objective

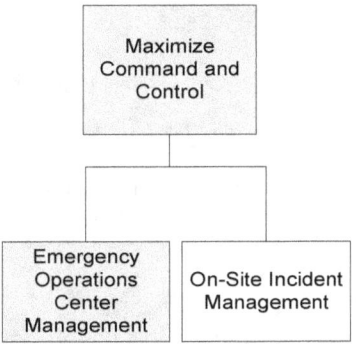

Emergency Operations Center Management

Definition: Emergency Operations Center Management is the location where all functional requirements are identified and supported.

0- None

1- Established doctrine (guidance, tactics, tasks, and procedures) for activating
        EOC (Emergency Operations Center)
        MACC (Multi-Agency Command Center)
        IOF (Initial Operating Facility)
    Information consolidation
    Issue processing
    Demobilization

2- Established command and control structure, with roles and responsibilities defined.

3- Direct emergency operation center's tactical operations.
Plans/doctrine are easily accessible and understood by personnel.
Ability to execute plans is present.

4- Exercise and validate plans.
All personnel formally trained.

5- Ability to monitor current operations in order to obtain feedback to reassess and improve current doctrine and organization.

Score	Values
0	0
1	27
2	48
3	69
4	90
5	100

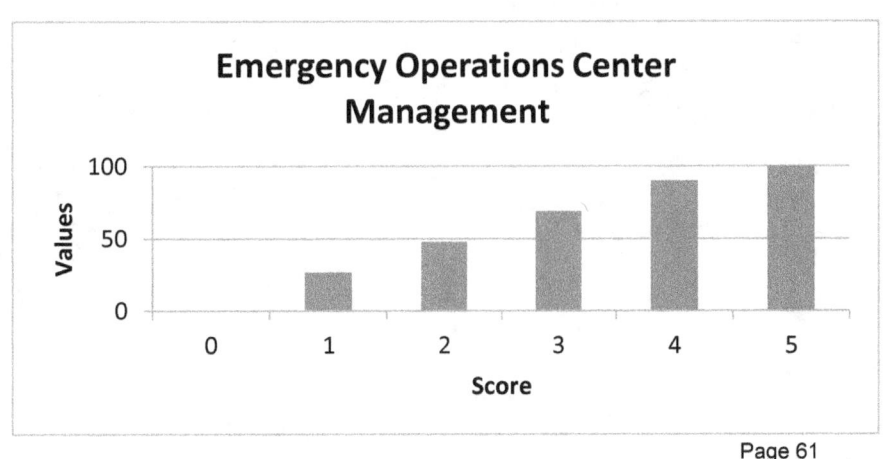

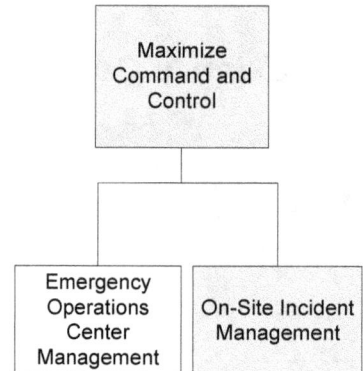

On-Site Incident Management

Definition: Onsite Incident Management determines the initial response after an incident. It establishes communication, command and control, resource allocation, initial assessments, and overall execution.

0- None

1- Established doctrine (guidance, tactics, tasks, and procedures):
      Resource management
      Incident action plan (IAP)
      Demobilization

2- Established command and control structure, with roles and responsibilities defined.

3- Direct on-site incident management.
Plans/doctrine are easily accessible and understood by personnel.
Ability to execute plans.

4- Exercise and validate plans.
All personnel formally trained.

5- Ability to monitor current operations in order to obtain feedback to reassess and improve current doctrine and organization.

Score	Values
0	0
1	23
2	47
3	73
4	90
5	100

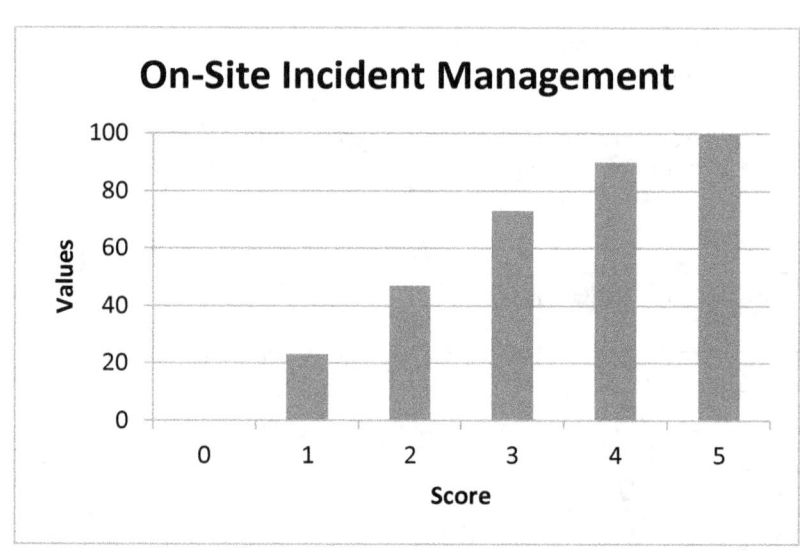

Appendix L
Maximize Incident Response Objective

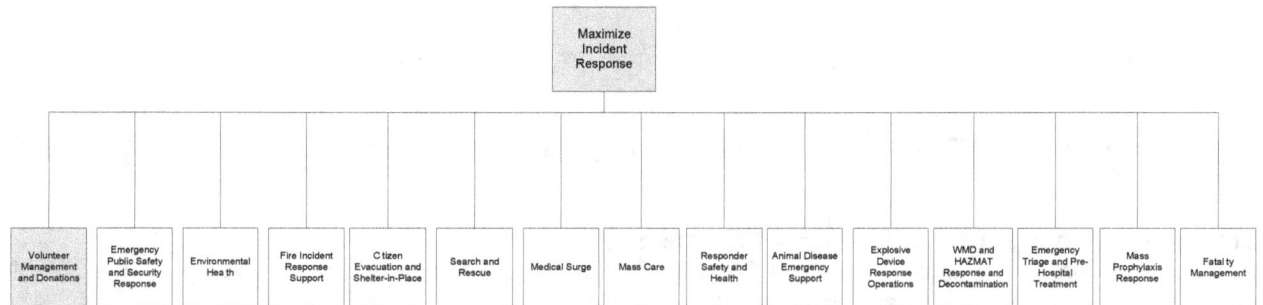

Volunteer Management and Donations

Definition: Volunteer Management and Donations is the coordination and organization of volunteers and all resources donated.

0- None

1- Established doctrine (guidance, tactics, tasks, and procedures):
   Establish warehouses and materials handling equipment
   Organize volunteers and assign them to disaster relief efforts
   Collect and manage material and cash donations
   Distribute donations

2- Established command and control structure, with roles and responsibilities defined.

3- Direct volunteer management operations.
   Plans/doctrine are easily accessible and understood by personnel.
   Ability to execute plans is present.

4- Exercise and validate plans.
   All personnel formally trained.

5- Ability to monitor current operations in order to obtain feedback to reassess and improve current doctrine and organization.

Score	Values
0	0
1	37
2	58
3	77
4	90
5	100

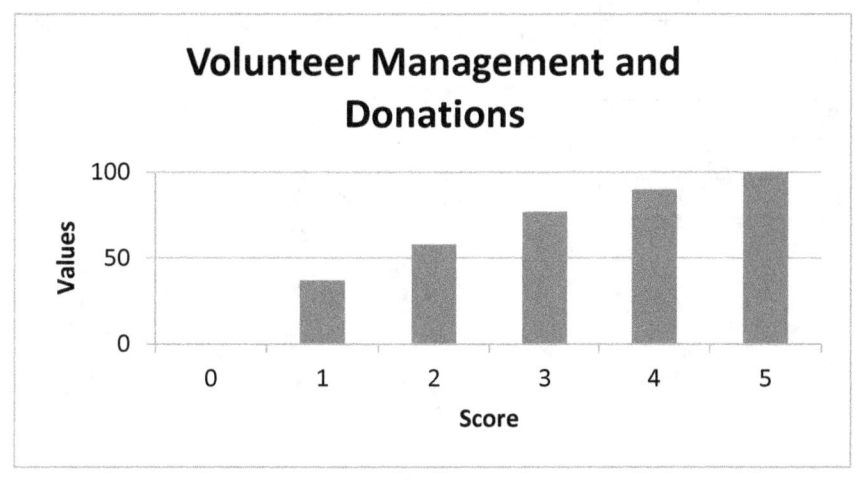

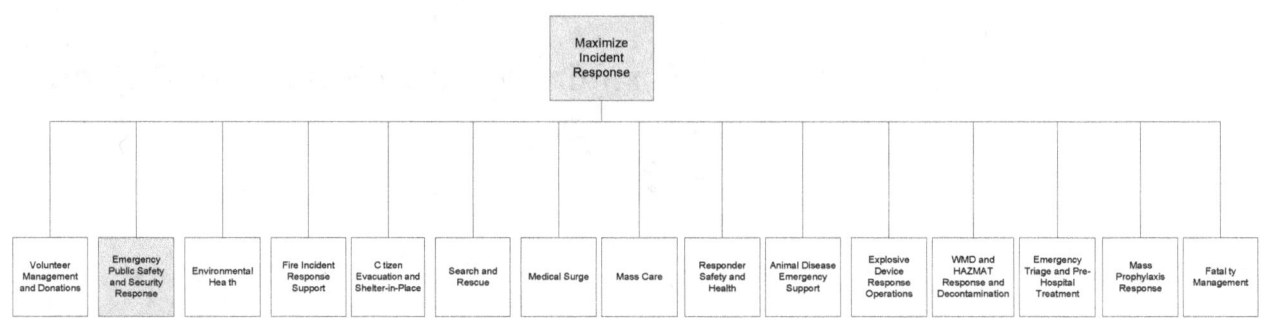

Emergency Public Safety and Security Response

Definition: Emergency Public Safety and Security Response are the assessment and operations for all safety requirements in an incident location.

0- None

1- Established doctrine (guidance, tactics, tasks, and procedures):
    Assess the incident scene and secure the area
    Control traffic, crowd, and scene
    Conduct law enforcement operations
    Manage criminal justice population (law enforcement)

2- Established command and control structure, with roles and responsibilities defined.

3- Direct public safety and security response operations.
Plans/doctrine are easily accessible and understood by personnel.
Ability to execute plans is present.

4- Exercise and validate plans.
All personnel formally trained.

5- Ability to monitor current operations in order to obtain feedback to reassess and improve current doctrine and organization.

Score	Values
0	0
1	29
2	45
3	62
4	85
5	100

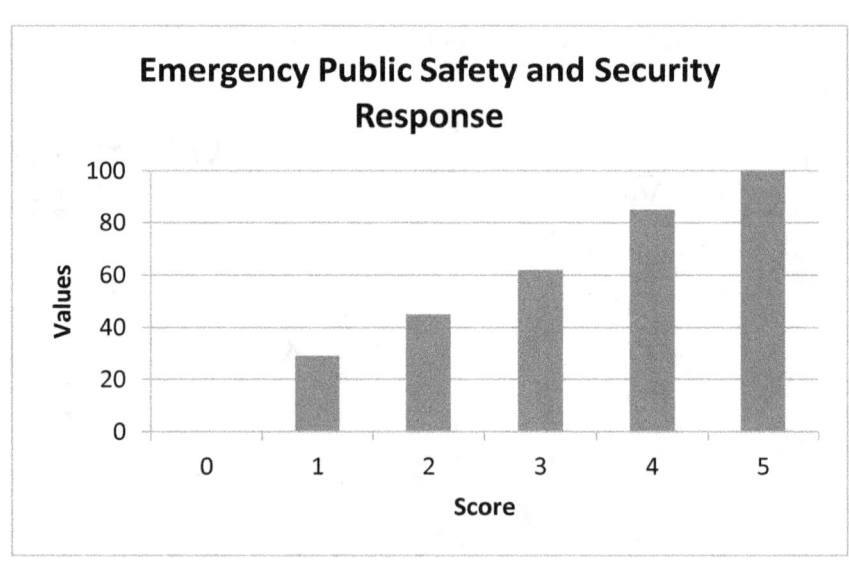

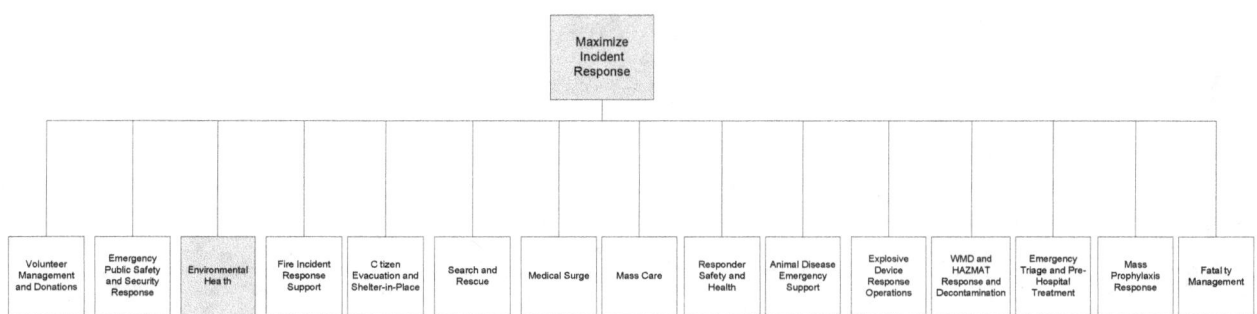

Environmental Health

Definition: Environmental Health encompasses all of the precautionary measures taken to ensure the public is safe from environmental hazards.

0- None

1- Established doctrine (guidance, tactics, tasks, and procedures):
        Secure and distribute
                Portable water supplies
                Food supplies
        Manage
                Wastewater
                Building environments
                Outdoor environments
                Solid waste/debris removal
                Mass care response
        Identify potential vectors and provide surveillance

2- Established command and control structure, with roles and responsibilities defined.

3- Direct environmental health operations.
Plans/doctrine are easily accessible and understood by personnel.
Ability to execute plans is present.

4- Exercise and validate plans.
All personnel formally trained.

5- Ability to monitor current operations in order to obtain feedback to reassess and improve current doctrine and organization.

Score	Values
0	0
1	34
2	50
3	68
4	88
5	100

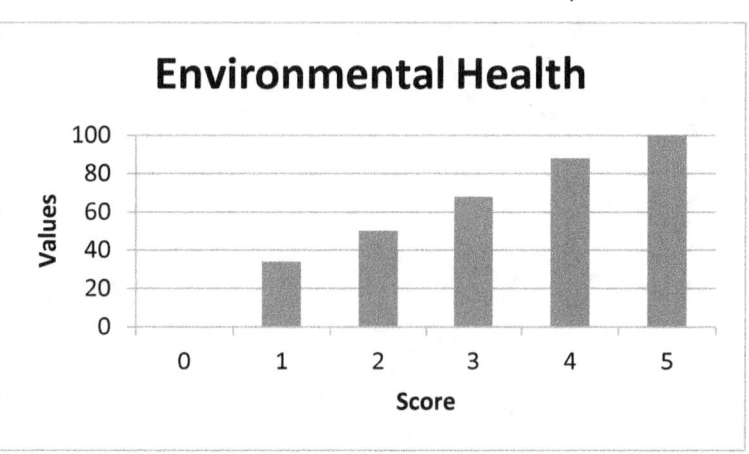

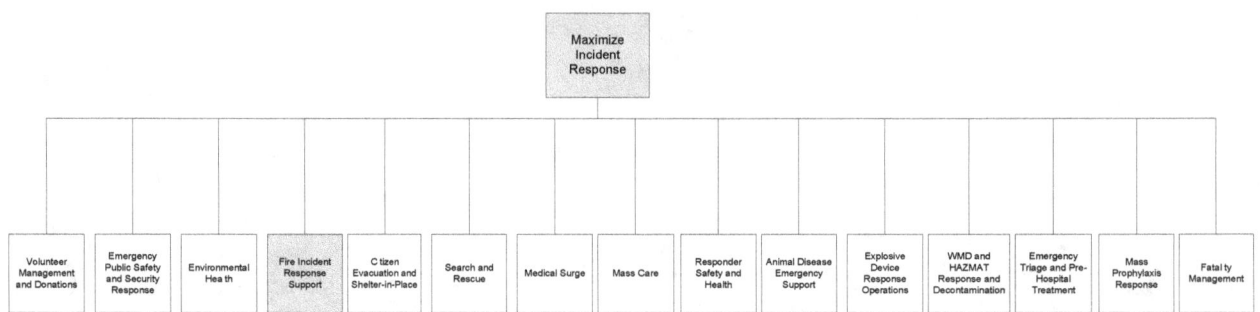

Fire Incident Response Support

Definition: Fire Incident Response Support are operations to respond to a major fire.

0- None

1- Established doctrine (guidance, tactics, tasks, and procedures):
    Search and rescue operations
    Scene forensics (assessing, characterizing, and investigating)

2- Established command and control structure, with roles and responsibilities defined.

3- Direct fire incident response support tactical operations.
    Plans/doctrine are easily accessible and understood by personnel.
    Ability to execute plans is present.

4- Exercise and validate plans.
    All personnel formally trained.

5- Ability to monitor current operations in order to obtain feedback to reassess and improve current doctrine and organization.

Score	Values
0	0
1	33
2	50
3	68
4	88
5	100

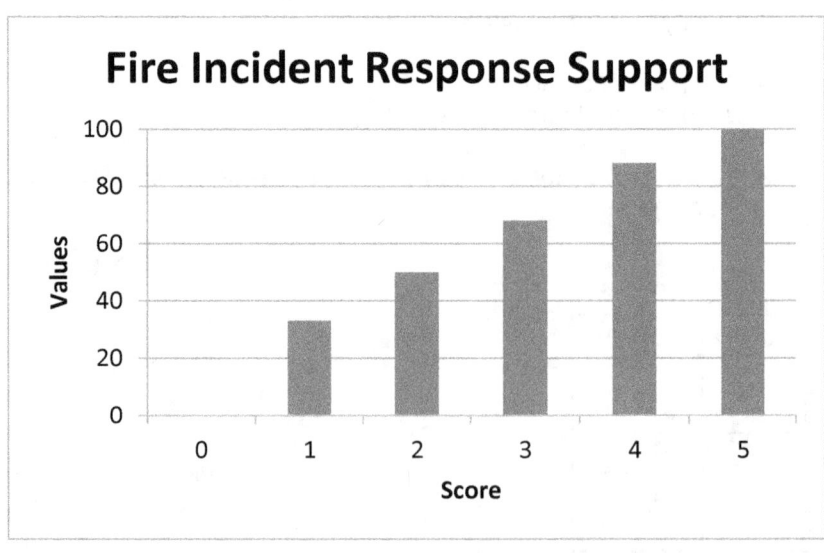

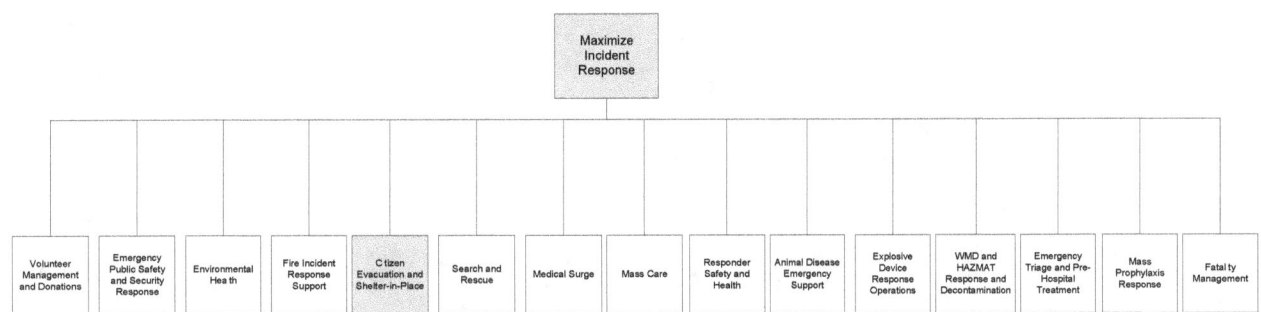

Citizen Evacuation and Shelter-in-place

Definition: Citizen Evacuation and Shelter-In-Place are the plans and procedures for evacuating and if necessary providing in place shelter for the affected population.

0- None

1- Established doctrine (guidance, tactics, tasks, and procedures):
      Implement evacuation orders to general population
      Collect and evaluate population requiring assistance
      Operate evacuation staging and reception areas
      Manage incoming evacuees
      Implement in-place protection procedures
      Manage re-entry into affected area

2- Established command and control structure, with roles and responsibilities defined.

3- Direct evacuation and/or in-place protection tactical operations.
Plans/doctrine are easily accessible and understood by personnel.
Ability to execute plans is present.

4- Exercise and validate plans.
All personnel formally trained.

5- Ability to monitor current operations in order to obtain feedback to reassess and improve current doctrine and organization.

Score	Values
0	0
1	28
2	48
3	68
4	89
5	100

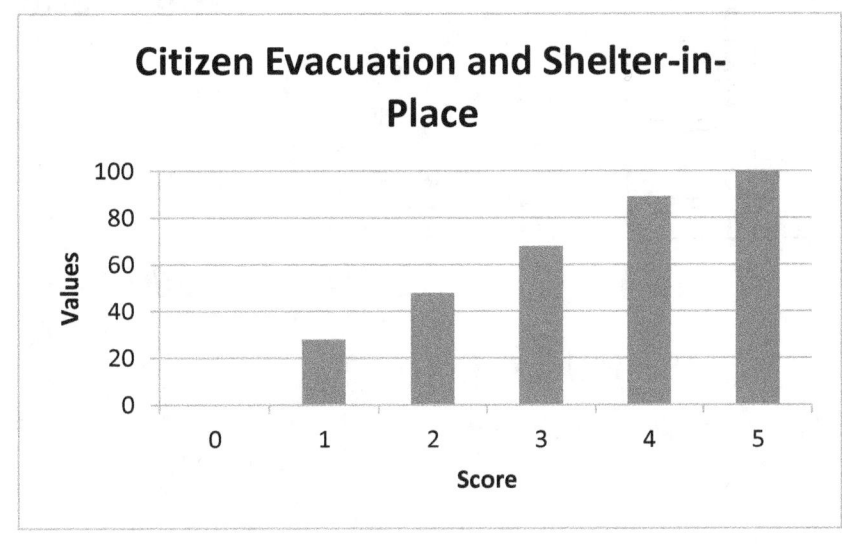

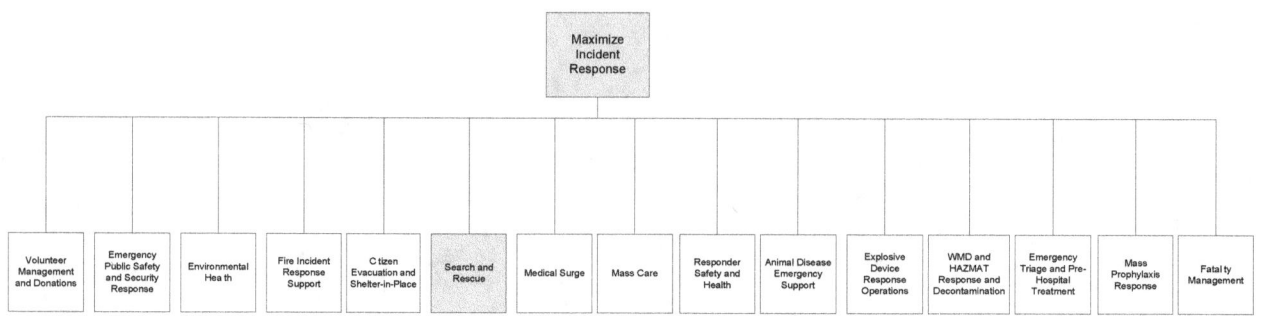

Search and Rescue

Definition: Search and Rescue are the procedures established to conduct any search and rescue operation for victims.

0- None

1- Established doctrine (guidance, tactics, tasks, and procedures):
        Conduct search operations
        Conduct rescue operations
        Provide medical treatment throughout rescue operation

2- Established command and control structure, with roles and responsibilities defined.

3- Direct search and rescue tactical operations.
Plans/doctrine are easily accessible and understood by personnel.
Ability to execute plans is present.

4- Exercise and validate plans.
All personnel formally trained.

5- Ability to monitor current operations in order to obtain feedback to reassess and improve current doctrine and organization.

Score	Values
0	0
1	28
2	48
3	72
4	89
5	100

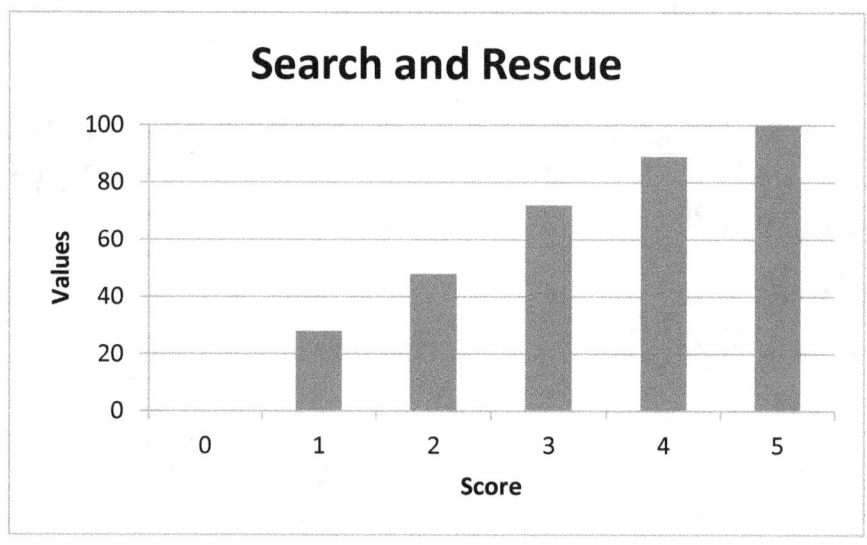

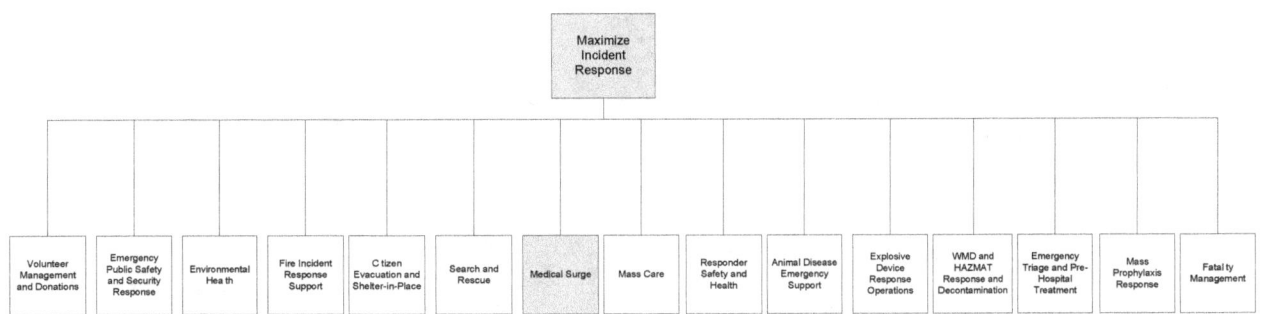

Medical Surge

Definition: Medical Surge is the massing of medical capability (equipment, personnel) to designated areas for medical treatment of mass casualties.

- 0- None

- 1- Established doctrine (guidance, tactics, tasks, and procedures):
      Establish medical logistical plan (equipment, personnel)
      Implement mass staffing procedures
      Implement mass equipment procedures
      Implement mass patient transfer procedures
      Receive and treat mass casualties

- 2- Established command and control structure, with roles and responsibilities defined.

- 3- Direct medical surge tactical operations.
     Plans/doctrine are easily accessible and understood by personnel.
     Ability to execute plans is present.

- 4- Exercise and validate plans.
     All personnel formally trained.

- 5- Ability to monitor current operations in order to obtain feedback to reassess and improve current doctrine and organization.

Score	Values
0	0
1	32
2	47
3	68
4	90
5	100

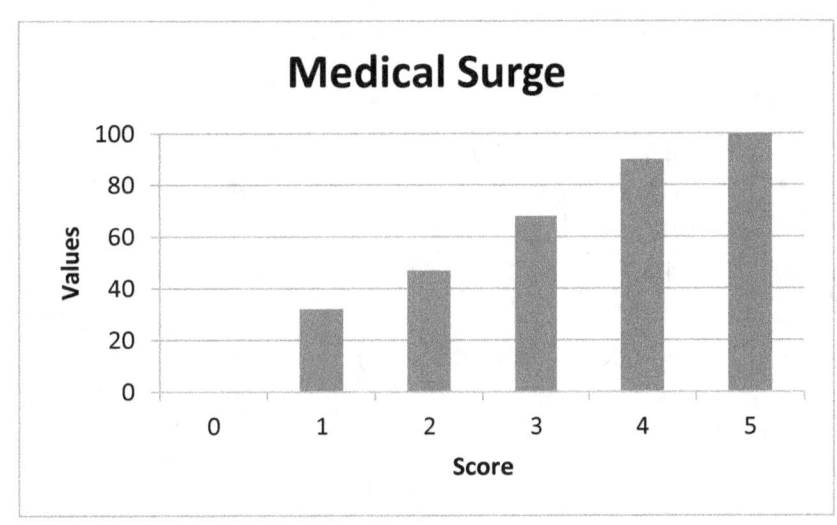

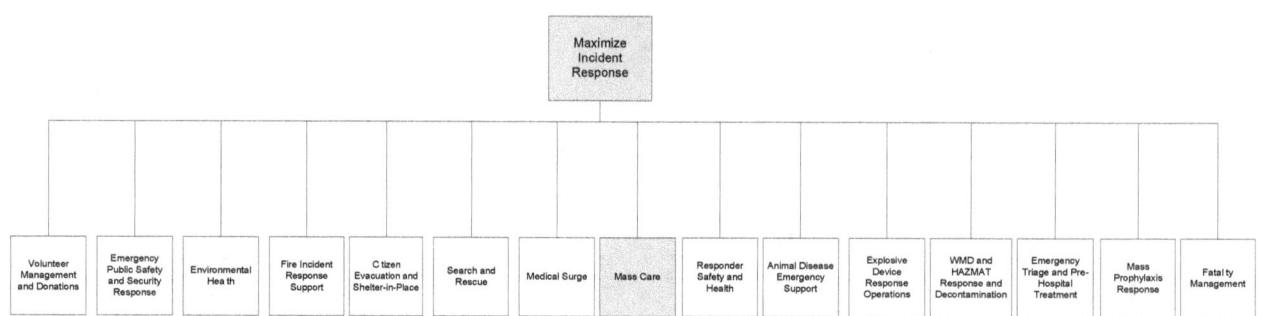

Mass Care

Definition: Mass Care is the overall shelter and food distribution operations for the general population and companion animals.

0- None

1- Established doctrine (guidance, tactics, tasks, and procedures):
      Establish logistical plan
      Establish bulk distribution operations
      Prepare and distribute food
      Establish shelter operations (general population, companion animals)

2- Established command and control structure, with roles and responsibilities defined.

3- Direct mass care operations.
Plans/doctrine are easily accessible and understood by personnel.
Ability to execute plans is present.

4- Exercise and validate plans.
All personnel formally trained.

5- Ability to monitor current operations in order to obtain feedback to reassess and improve current doctrine and organization.

Score	Values
0	0
1	33
2	45
3	62
4	84
5	100

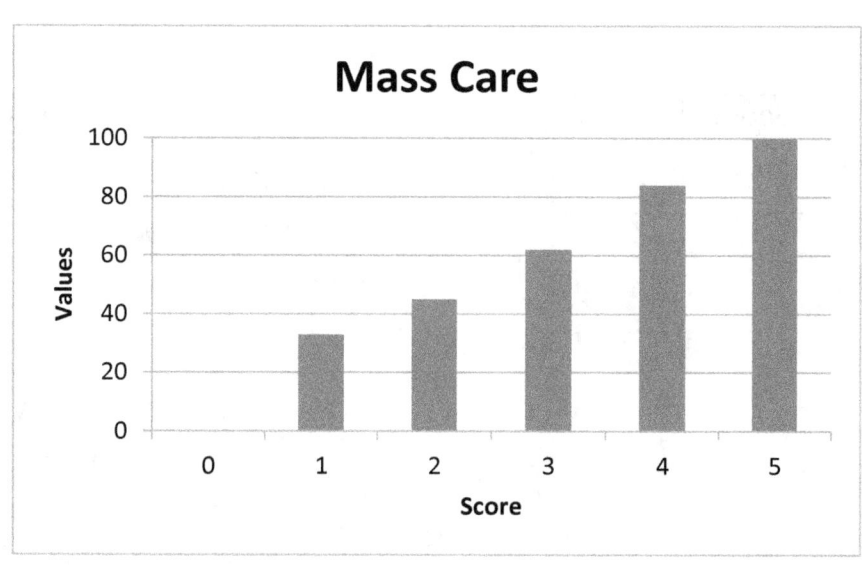

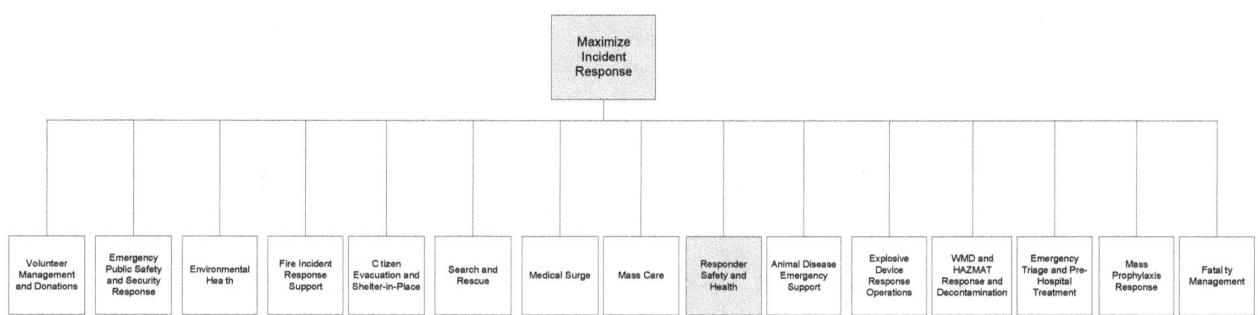

Responder Safety and Health

Definition: Ability to monitor the safety and protect responders from health risks.

0- None

1- Established doctrine (guidance, tactics, tasks, and procedures):
    Identify safety/PPE (personal protective equipment) needs
    Distribute PPE
    React to responder's needs

2- Established command and control structure, with roles and responsibilities defined.

3- Direct responder safety and health tactical operations.
Plans/doctrine are easily accessible and understood by personnel.
Ability to execute plans is present.

4- Exercise and validate plans.
All personnel formally trained.

5- Ability to monitor current operations in order to obtain feedback to reassess and improve current doctrine and organization.

Score	Values
0	0
1	28
2	42
3	70
4	89
5	100

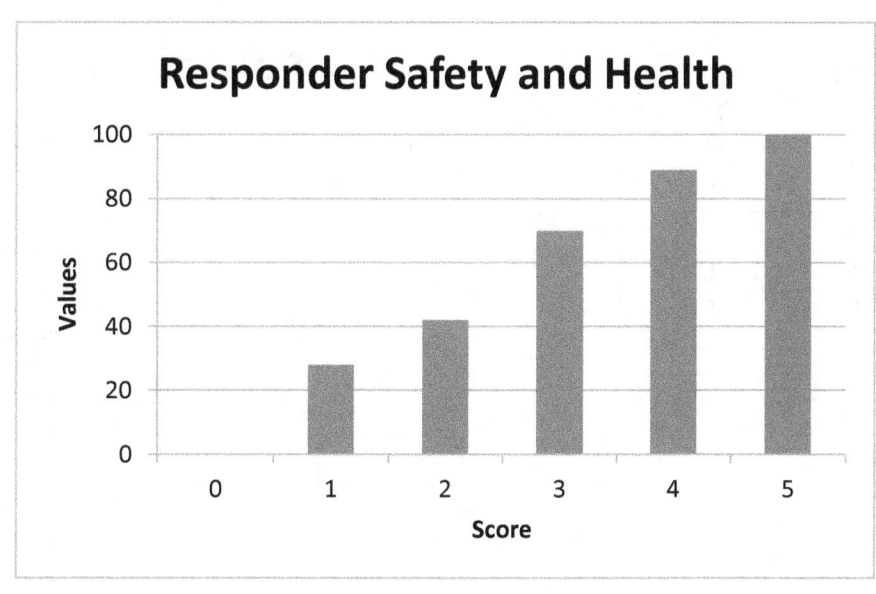

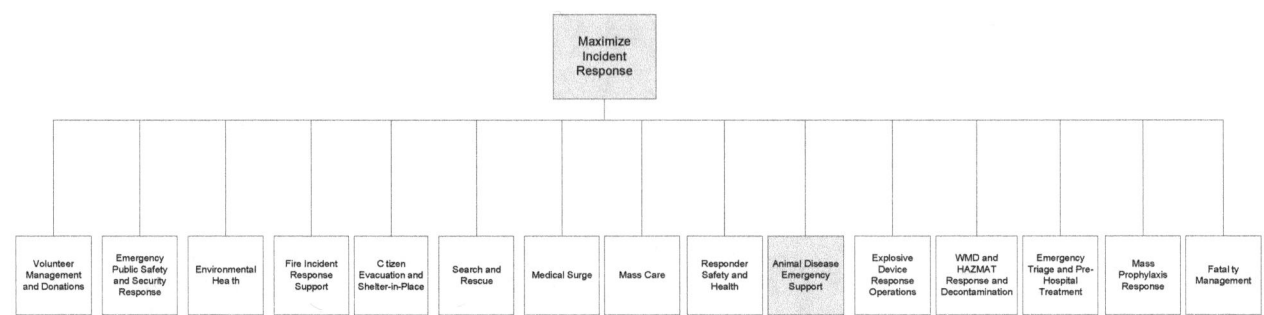

Animal Disease Emergency Support

Definition: Ability to monitor animal health, contain disease outbreaks, and establish euthanasia and disposal.

0- None

1- Established doctrine (guidance, tactics, tasks, and procedures):
    Conduct animal health epidemiological investigation and surveillance
    Implement disease containment measures
    Conduct animal euthanasia and disposal

2- Established command and control structure, with roles and responsibilities defined.

3- Direct animal disease emergency support tactical operations.
Plans/doctrine are easily accessible and understood by personnel.
Ability to execute plans is present.

4- Exercise and validate plans.
All personnel formally trained.

5- Ability to monitor current operations in order to obtain feedback to reassess and improve current doctrine and organization.

Score	Values
0	0
1	28
2	43
3	60
4	79
5	100

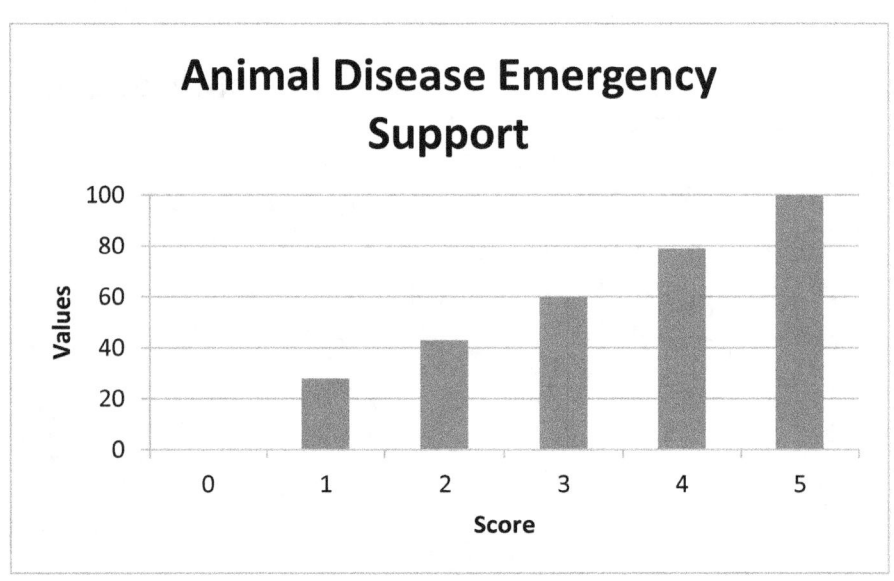

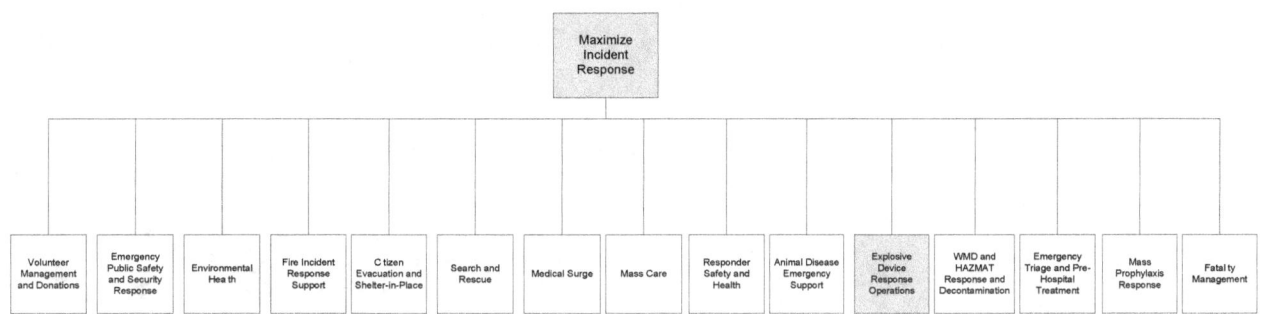

Explosive Device Response Operations

Definition: Identify, recover, remove, and transport explosive material from site to disposal location.

0- None

1- Established doctrine (guidance, tactics, tasks, and procedures):
        Identify explosive material
        Secure site
        Removal and transport of explosive material
        Disposal of explosive material
        Clear site (safe)

2- Established command and control structure, with roles and responsibilities defined.

3- Direct explosive device response operations.
Plans/doctrine are easily accessible and understood by personnel.
Ability to execute plans is present.

4- Exercise and validate plans.
All personnel formally trained.

5- Ability to monitor current operations in order to obtain feedback to reassess and improve current doctrine and organization.

Score	Values
0	0
1	38
2	53
3	69
4	89
5	100

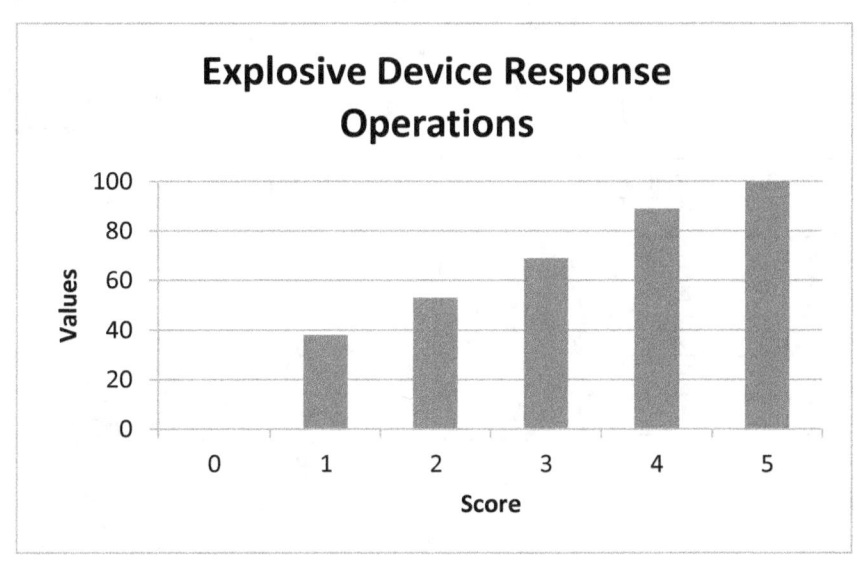

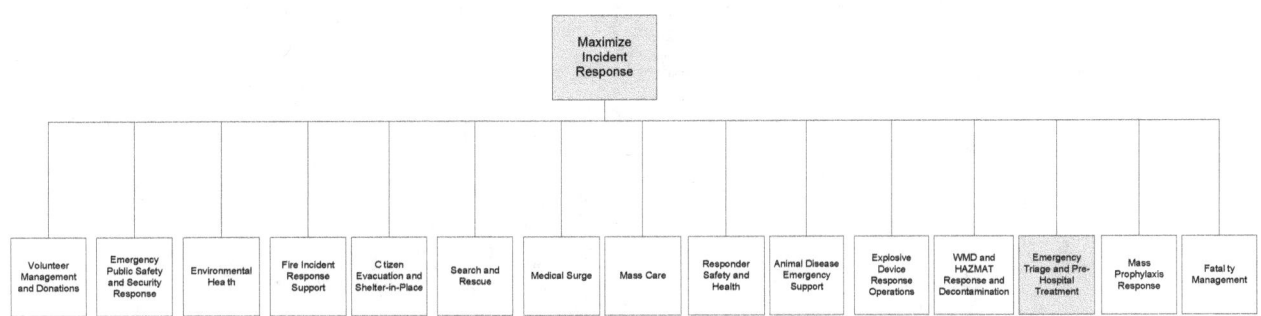

Emergency Triage and Pre-Hospital Treatment

Definition: Prioritizing casualties and providing initial treatment at incident site and during transportation to a medical treatment facility.

0-   None

1-   Established doctrine (guidance, tactics, tasks, and procedures):
        Conduct triage
        Conduct pre-hospital treatment
        Conduct treatment during ambulatory transport

2-   Established command and control structure, with roles and responsibilities defined.

3-   Direct triage and pre-hospital treatment tactical operations.
Plans/doctrine are easily accessible and understood by personnel.
Ability to execute plans is present.

4-   Exercise and validate plans.
All personnel formally trained.

5-   Ability to monitor current operations in order to obtain feedback to reassess and improve current doctrine and organization.

Score	Values
0	0
1	40
2	55
3	69
4	89
5	100

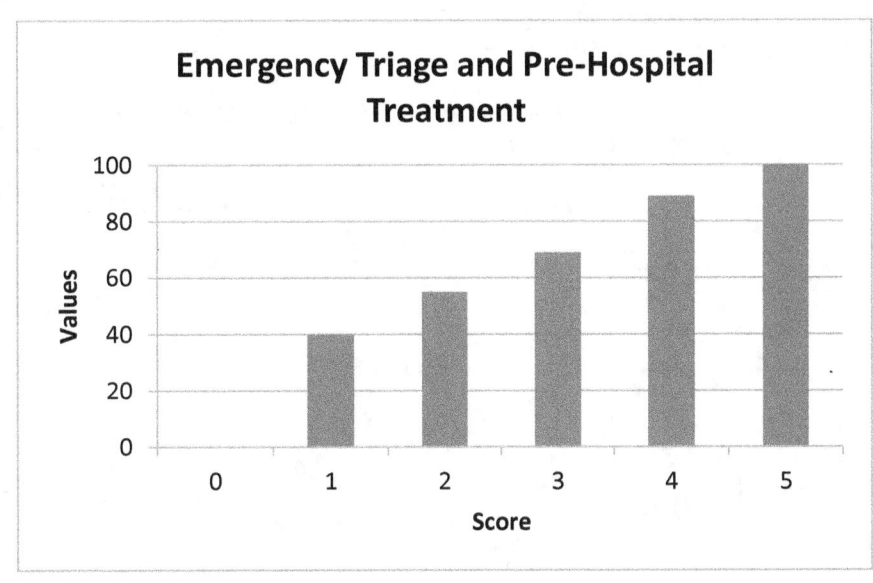

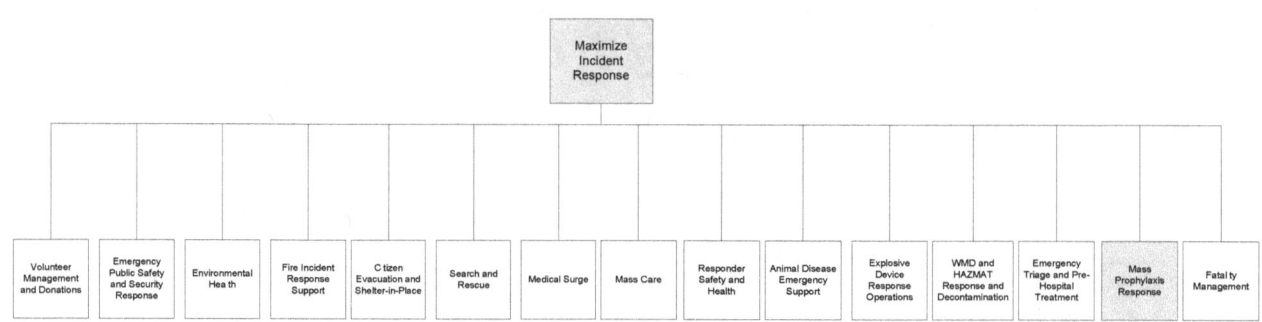

Mass Prophylaxis Response

Definition: Ability to respond to a large outbreak of disease or sickness through the ability to contain, treat, and monitor the outbreak by isolation, quarantine, and treatment of victims.

0- None

1- Established doctrine (guidance, tactics, tasks, and procedures):
        Establish a logistical plan
        Isolate area
        Quarantine people and animals
        Implement additional restrictions

2- Established command and control structure, with roles and responsibilities defined.

3- Plans/doctrine are easily accessible and understood by personnel.
Direct mass prophylaxis tactical operations.
        Ability to execute plans is present.
            Conduct medical screening

            Establish points for dispensing medications
            Conduct triage for symptoms
            Mass distribution of medical treatment and supplies

4- Exercise and validate plans.
All personnel formally trained.

5- Ability to monitor current operations in order to obtain feedback to reassess and improve current doctrine and organization.

Score	Values
0	0
1	33
2	45
3	67
4	89
5	100

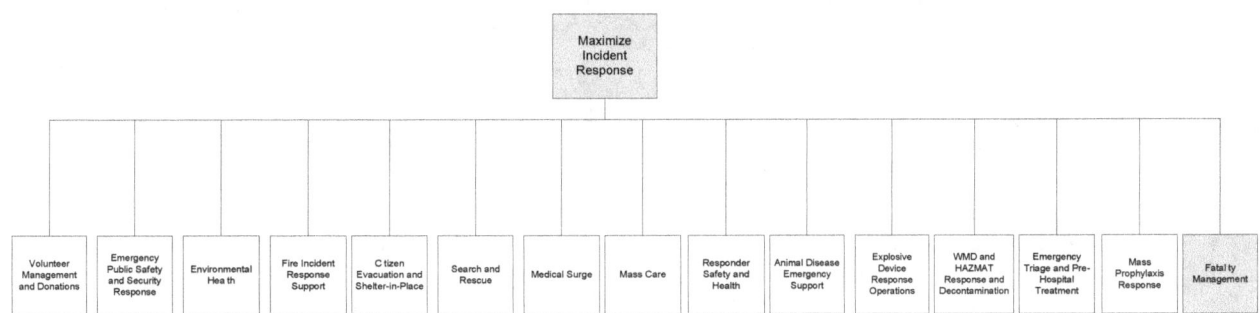

Fatality Management

Definition: Manage and control fatalities and conduct morgue operations in support of a major incident.

0- None

1- Established doctrine (guidance, tactics, tasks, and procedures):
        Conduct on-scene fatality management operations
        Conduct morgue operations
            Ante mortem data
            Victim identification
            Family notification
            Final disposal

2- Established command and control structure, with roles and responsibilities defined.

3- Direct fatality management tactical operations.
Plans/doctrine are easily accessible and understood by personnel.
Ability to execute plans is present.

4- Exercise and validate plans.
All personnel formally trained.

5- Ability to monitor current operations in order to obtain feedback to reassess and improve current doctrine and organization.

Score	Values
0	0
1	33
2	45
3	67
4	89
5	100

This Page Intentionally Left Blank

Appendix M
Maximize Resource Management Objective

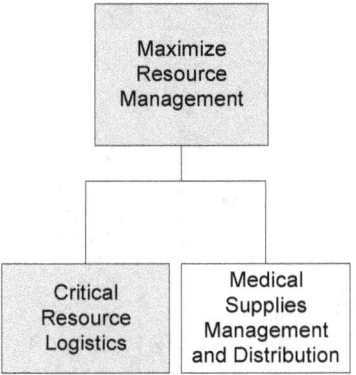

Critical Resource Logistics

Definition: Critical resources are facilities, transportation, supplies, equipment, maintenance, fueling, food service, and communications utilized to support incident response and operations, which measures the effectiveness of the management and distribution of these resources.

0- None

1- Established doctrine (guidance, tactics, tasks, and procedures):
      Establish critical resource logistics plan
          Respond to needs assessment and inventory
          Acquire resources
          Transport, track, and manage resources
          Maintain and recover resources

2- Established command and control structure, with roles and responsibilities defined.

3- Direct critical resource logistics operations.
Plans/doctrine are easily accessible and understood by personnel.
Ability to execute plans is present.

4- Exercise and validate plans.
All personnel formally trained.

5- Ability to monitor current operations in order to obtain feedback to reassess and improve current doctrine and organization.

Score	Values
0	0
1	33
2	48
3	63
4	89
5	100

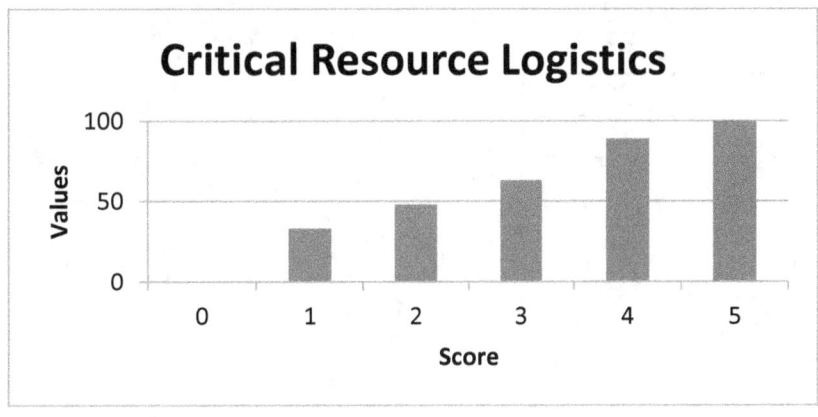

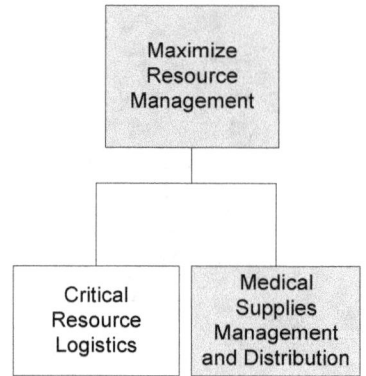

Medical Supply Management and Distribution

Definition: The distribution, management, and recovery of medical resources.

0- None

1- Established doctrine (guidance, tactics, tasks, and procedures):
        Establish medical supply logistic plan
            Secure medical supplies
            Inventory, package, and distribute medical supplies
            Recover excess medical supplies

2- Established command and control structure, with roles and responsibilities defined.

3- Direct medical supply management and distribution tactical operations.
Plans/doctrine are easily accessible and understood by personnel.
Ability to execute plans is present.

4- Exercise and validate plans.
All personnel formally trained.

5- Ability to monitor current operations in order to obtain feedback to reassess and improve current doctrine and organization.

Score	Values
0	0
1	35
2	48
3	63
4	89
5	100

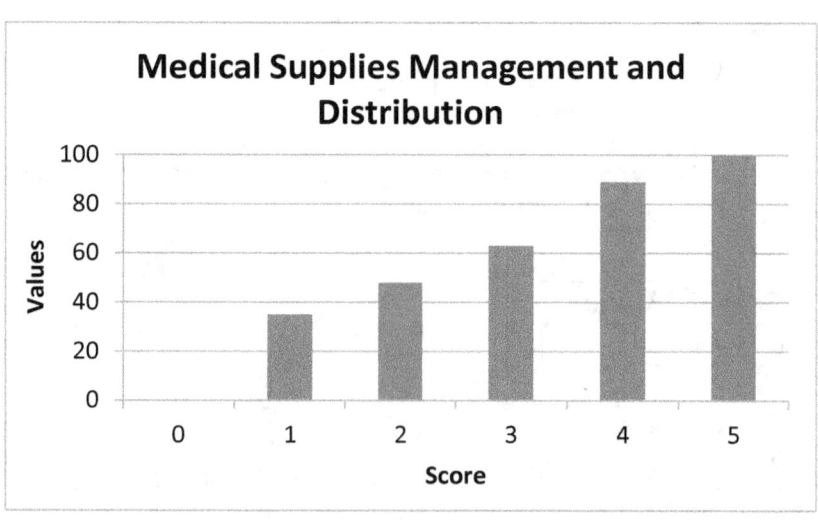

Appendix N
Partner Nation Evaluation Model User Guide

N.1 Directions
Begin Partner Nation Evaluation
1. To begin your assessment of the Partner Nation, click on the "Multiple User Inputs" button if there are multiple evaluations or click on the "Input Partner Nation Score" button for a single user evaluation on home page.
2. The "Multiple Input" page allows for 10 users to input scores for each value measure over the period of 10 days.
3. The average of all the inputs from the "Multiple Input" page can be pasted into the "Input Partner Nation Scores" page and the evaluation will be populated.
4. The partner nation score is broken down into 26 different value measures.
5. Each value measure has a score scale from 0-5 and an associated description of how a Partner Nation can achieve a score.
6. Each number on the scale is cumulative meaning that each number builds on the one previous to it. For example, in order to score a 3, the criteria from both 1 and 2 on the scale must be met.
7. All criteria must be met in order to score the full point.
8. When at least one of the criteria for a number are met, half a point can be rewarded. For example, if a score of 3 requires 5 criteria, and the partner nation has only 2 of the 5 met, they can receive 2.5 points
9. Once a value measure has been given a score of 0-5, the score will be inputted into column D.
10. Once the scores have been inputted click "Home" and then click on the "Go to Partner Nation Evaluation" button. This will take you to the evaluation page which will include the overall Partner Nation score and a set of graphs displaying the breakdown of the data.

Model Adjustments
1. To adjust the model swing weights click on the "Input Value Measure and Objective Weights" button.
2. If a value measure or objective is determined to be more important or produces a greater value than originally assigned the swing weights can be changed on this page.
3. To change the objective's swing weights insert swing weight from 0-100 in column C. To change the value measure's swing weights insert the weight from 0-100 in column F.
4. Changes to the swing weight will either increase or decrease the importance of that particular value measure or objective.
5. The "Calculations" page shows all of the internal calculations of the model using the scores and swing weights.

Objectives and Value Measures
1. These seven buttons correspond with the seven objective categories. Each objective page displays a value measure with its definition and respective scale descriptions as well as a graph that displays the value associated with each score on the scale.
2. On this page, the values for each scale score can be changed if needed. Over time if certain criteria of a value measure become more important or hold more value, than its value can be changed by changing the number in the column next to the scale.
3. The number inputted must be between 0-100. Upon inputting these numbers the weight of the value measure scale will be changed on the main model.
4. Also in the top left corner of each value measure box, there is a score box where the value measure's score can be inputted.

N.2 Pages
Input Page

To begin an evaluation, the user will give each value measure a score ranging from 0 to 5 based on the scale for that value measure. There are two ways to run the evaluation correctly. If there are multiple personnel inputting data that has been collected over a period of time, they will begin by putting all of the data into the "Multiple Inputs" page in the model. If there is only one person collecting data for a partner nation, they will enter the data directly into the "Input Scores" page of the model. The purpose of the "Multiple Inputs" page is to get an average score for each of the value measures so that the data collected during the engagement is not reliant on a single user's evaluation.

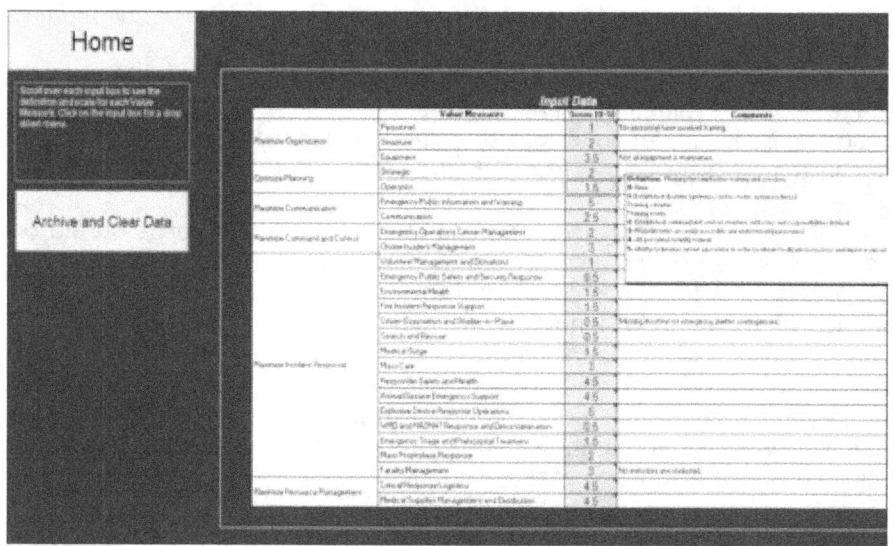

Figure N.1 *"Input Scores" Page*

Engagement Location Average Scores from 10 users over a period of 10 days		Day 1	Day 2	Day 3	Day 4	Day 5	Day 6	Day 7	Day 8	Day 9	Day 10	Average
	Value Measures	Day 1	Day 2	Day 3	Day 4	Day 5	Day 6	Day 7	Day 8	Day 9	Day 10	**Average**
Maximize Organization	Personnel	1.0	1.0	1.0	1.0	1.0	1.0	1.0	1.0	1.0	1.0	**1.0**
	Structure	2.0	2.0	2.0	2.0	2.0	2.0	2.0	2.0	2.0	2.0	**2.0**
	Equipment	3.5	3.5	3.5	3.5	3.5	3.5	3.5	3.5	3.5	3.5	**3.5**
Optimize Planning	Strategic	2.0	2.0	2.0	2.0	2.0	2.0	2.0	2.0	2.0	2.0	**2.0**
	Operation	1.5	1.5	1.5	1.5	1.5	1.5	1.5	1.5	1.5	1.5	**1.5**
Maximize Communication	Emergency Public Information and Warning	5.0	5.0	5.0	5.0	5.0	5.0	5.0	5.0	5.0	5.0	**5.0**
	Communication	2.5	2.5	2.5	2.5	2.5	2.5	2.5	2.5	2.5	2.5	**2.5**
Maximize Command and Control	Emergency Operations Center Management	2.0	2.0	2.0	2.0	2.0	2.0	2.0	2.0	2.0	2.0	**2.0**
	Onsite Incident Management	3.0	3.0	3.0	3.0	3.0	3.0	3.0	3.0	3.0	3.0	**3.0**
Maximize Incident Response	Volunteer Management and Donations	1.0	1.0	1.0	1.0	1.0	1.0	1.0	1.0	1.0	1.0	**1.0**
	Emergency Public Safety and Security Response	0.5	0.5	0.5	0.5	0.5	0.5	0.5	0.5	0.5	0.5	**0.5**
	Environmental Health	1.5	1.5	1.5	1.5	1.5	1.5	1.5	1.5	1.5	1.5	**1.5**
	Fire Incident Response Support	1.5	1.5	1.5	1.5	1.5	1.5	1.5	1.5	1.5	1.5	**1.5**
	Citizen Evacuation and Shelter-in-Place	0.5	0.5	0.5	0.5	0.5	0.5	0.5	0.5	0.5	0.5	**0.5**
	Search and Rescue	0.5	0.5	0.5	0.5	0.5	0.5	0.5	0.5	0.5	0.5	**0.5**
	Medical Surge	1.5	1.5	1.5	1.5	1.5	1.5	1.5	1.5	1.5	1.5	**1.5**
	Mass Care	3.0	3.0	3.0	3.0	3.0	3.0	3.0	3.0	3.0	3.0	**3.0**
	Responder Safety and Health	4.5	4.5	4.5	4.5	4.5	4.5	4.5	4.5	4.5	4.5	**4.5**
	Animal Disease Emergency Support	4.5	4.5	4.5	4.5	4.5	4.5	4.5	4.5	4.5	4.5	**4.5**
	Explosive Device Response Operations	5.0	5.0	5.0	5.0	5.0	5.0	5.0	5.0	5.0	5.0	**5.0**
	WMD and HAZMAT Response and Decontamination	0.5	0.5	0.5	0.5	0.5	0.5	0.5	0.5	0.5	0.5	**0.5**
	Emergency Triage and Prehospital Treatment	1.5	1.5	1.5	1.5	1.5	1.5	1.5	1.5	1.5	1.5	**1.5**
	Mass Prophylaxis Response	2.0	2.0	2.0	2.0	2.0	2.0	2.0	2.0	2.0	2.0	**2.0**
	Fatality Management	3.0	3.0	3.0	3.0	3.0	3.0	3.0	3.0	3.0	3.0	**3.0**
Maximize Resource Management	Critical Response Logistics	4.5	4.5	4.5	4.5	4.5	4.5	4.5	4.5	4.5	4.5	**4.5**
	Medical Supplies Management and Distribution	4.5	4.5	4.5	4.5	4.5	4.5	4.5	4.5	4.5	4.5	**4.5**

Figure N.2 *"Multiple Users Input" Page*

Calculations

Once the data for all of the value measures is placed into the "Input Scores" page, the calculations will run automatically and populate the weighted score for that value measure. The math behind the model begins by converting the raw data score into the value from the value measure tables. That value is then multiplied by the local objective weight that it falls under. That new value is then multiplied by the normalized weight of that individual value measure. For example, if a PN receives a score of four for the personnel value measure, it will receive a value of 85. However, this value is then multiplied by 14%, the normalized weight of the Maximize Organization objective. And lastly this value is multiplied by 6.5% for a final value of .7735. The same process will be used to find a value for all value measures. Following these multiplications, the individual values are summed together and divided by the ideal score to obtain the overall PN score out of 100.

Figure N.3 "Calculations" Page

Evaluation Page

The evaluation page of the model displays the Overall Partner Nation Score that stems from the user(s) inputs from their data collection. This score is measured out of a 100 and will give the user and stakeholders a summary of the PN's current consequence management capabilities and capacities. The evaluation page also allows DTRA to locate the deficient value measures and objectives for that PN. The bar chart and the radar diagrams display the actual score (what the country scored) and compares that to the ideal score (the best a country could have scored). Additionally, the evaluation page provides more traceability with the "Input Minimum Percentages" tables. With these tables, the stakeholders can establish a threshold or minimum percentage that the value measures and objectives must meet. If the value measures do not meet this baseline requirement, the underperforming component will appear red and allow the user to quickly locate the deficiency. This is depicted in Figures N.4 and N.5.

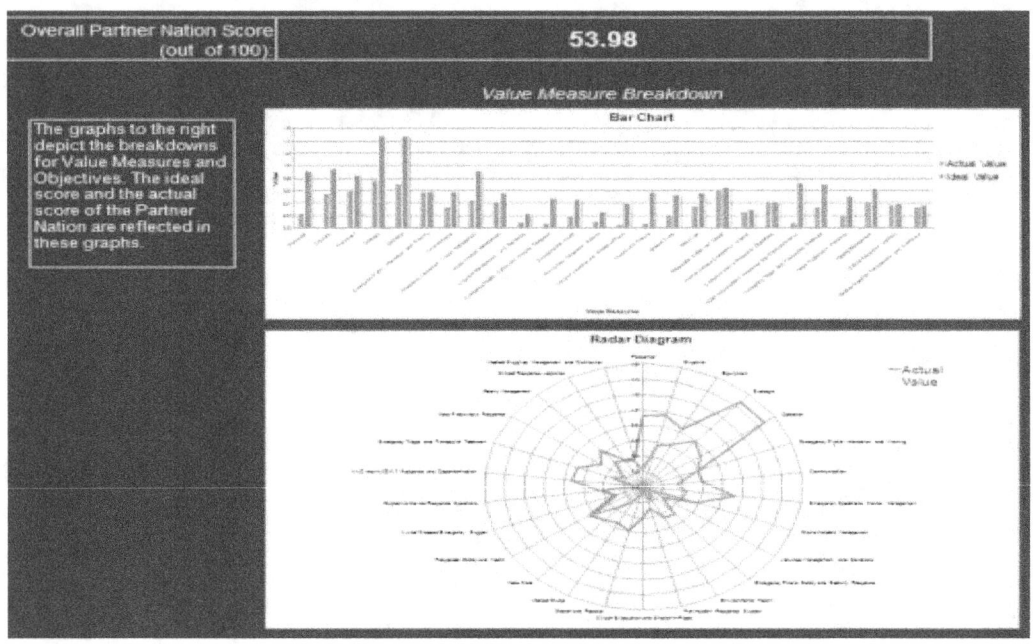

Figure N.4 *Evaluation Page – Bar Chart, Radar Diagram, and Overall Partner Nation Score*

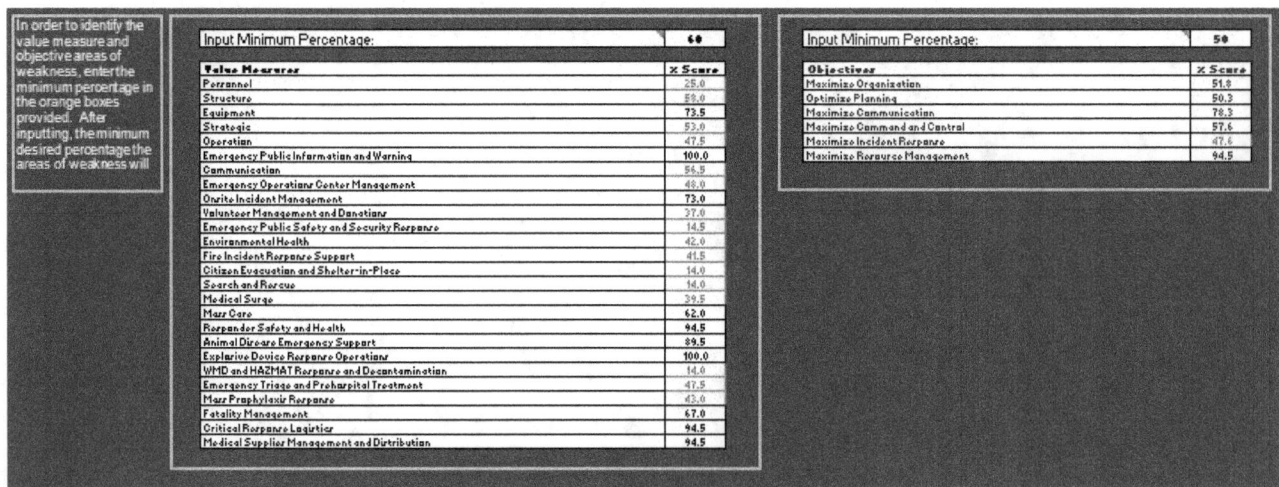

Figure N.5 *Evaluation Page – Minimum Input Percentage Tables*

Archive Page

The archive page of the model contains the data of previous evaluations. This page serves as the database for the Partner Nation Evaluation Model. It contains the date of the evaluation, the score that the PN achieved, the individual value measure scores, and any comments that the user might have inputted at that time. This page allows DTRA to track the progress of PNs and compare their capabilities and capacities over time.

<table>
<tr><td rowspan="2">Home</td><td colspan="3">Date</td><td>28-Feb-13</td><td colspan="3">Date</td><td>20-Feb-13</td></tr>
<tr><td colspan="3">PN Score</td><td>57.29</td><td colspan="3">PN Score</td><td>53.98</td></tr>
</table>

To add to the archives, go to the "Input Scores" Page and click the "Archive and Clear" button. Input the date after running the macro.

(Note: This page will not work if it is protected. Please do not change anything on this page. If you wish to copy any of the values archived, ensure you use Paste Special > Values).

Value Measures	Score (0-5)	Comments		Value Measures	Score (0-5)	Comments
Personnel	N/A	No personnel have received training.		Personnel	1.0	0
Structure	2.0	0		Structure	2.0	0
Equipment	3.5	Not all equipment is maintained.		Equipment	3.5	0
Strategic	2.0	0		Strategic	2.0	0
Operation	1.5	0		Operation	1.5	0
Emergency Public Information and Warning	5.0	0		Emergency Public Information and Warning	5.0	0
Communication	2.5	0		Communication	2.5	0
Emergency Operations Center Management	2.0	0		Emergency Operations Center Management	2.0	0
Onsite Incident Management	3.0	0		Onsite Incident Management	3.0	0
Volunteer Management and Donations	1.0	0		Volunteer Management and Donations	1.0	0
Emergency Public Safety and Security Response	0.5	0		Emergency Public Safety and Security Response	0.5	0
Environmental Health	1.5	0		Environmental Health	1.5	0
Fire Incident Response Support	1.5	0		Fire Incident Response Support	1.5	0
Citizen Evacuation and Shelter-in-Place	0.5	Missing doctrine for emergency shelter contingencies.		Citizen Evacuation and Shelter-in-Place	0.5	0
Search and Rescue	N/A	0		Search and Rescue	0.5	0
Medical Surge	1.5	0		Medical Surge	1.5	0
Mass Care	3.0	0		Mass Care	3.0	0
Responder Safety and Health	4.5	0		Responder Safety and Health	4.5	0
Animal Disease Emergency Support	4.5	0		Animal Disease Emergency Support	4.5	0
Explosive Device Response Operations	5.0	0		Explosive Device Response Operations	5.0	0
WMD and HAZMAT Response and Decontamination	0.5	0		WMD and HAZMAT Response and Decontamination	0.5	0
Emergency Triage and Prehospital Treatment	1.5	0		Emergency Triage and Prehospital Treatment	1.5	0
Mass Prophylaxis Response	2.0	0		Mass Prophylaxis Response	2.0	0
Fatality Management	3.0	No exercises are conducted.		Fatality Management	3.0	0
Critical Response Logistics	4.5	0		Critical Response Logistics	4.5	0
Medical Supplies Management and Distribution	4.5	0		Medical Supplies Management and Distribution	4.5	0

Figure N.6 "Archive" Page

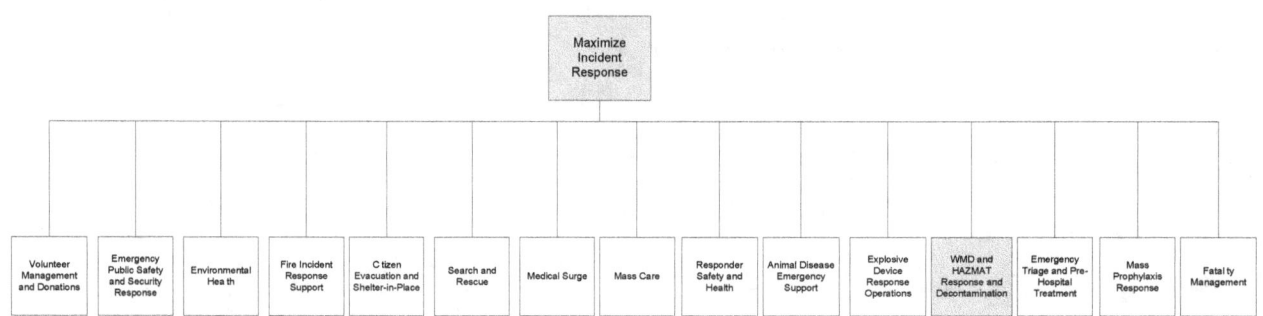

WMD and HAZMAT Response and Decontamination

Definition: Ability to identify, evaluate the risks, and remove WMD (weapons of mass destruction) or HAZMAT (hazardous material), to include decontamination of the site.

0- None

1- Established doctrine (guidance, tactics, tasks, and procedures):
    Identify and assess hazards of material
    Evaluate risks
    Remove material
    Decontaminate the site
    Conduct rescue operations if necessary
    Develop mitigation strategies

2- Established command and control structure, with roles and responsibilities defined.

3- Direct WMD and HAZMAT response and decontamination tactical operations.
    Plans/doctrine are easily accessible and understood by personnel.
    Ability to execute plans is present.

4- Exercise and validate plans.
    All personnel formally trained.

5- Ability to monitor current operations in order to obtain feedback to reassess and improve current doctrine and organization.

Score	Values
0	0
1	28
2	43
3	62
4	89
5	100

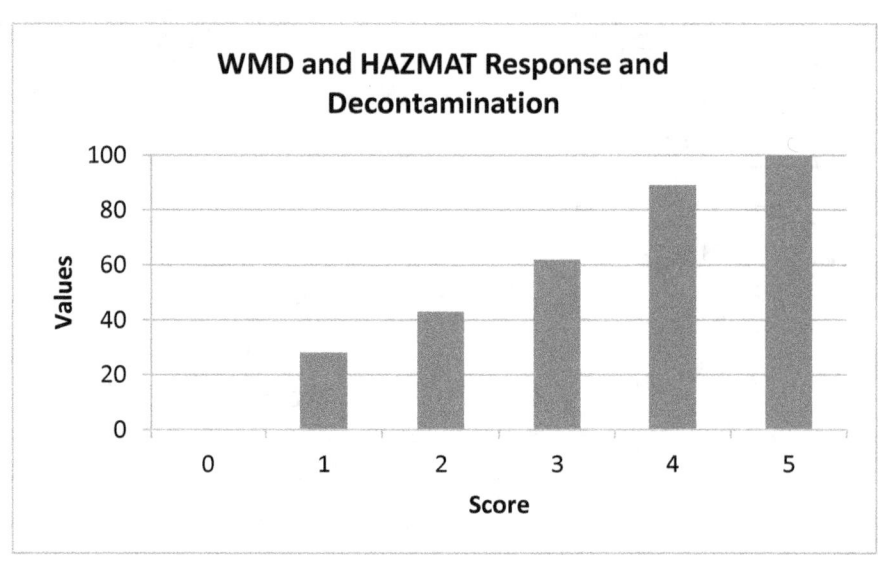